Michele Lee Browning

JUST ONE WORD

a Gateway to Inner Truths

Coloring Book For Everyone

VOLUME 3

Dedication

This book is dedicated to the memory
of my hero and mother, Peggy Browning,
who was a prime example of a survivor.
She was both an inspiration and a role model for me.
Rest in peace, my love, my friend.

Acknowledgement

Special thanks and gratitude to my family
and friends who always supported me in my Art and
encouraged me to begin this project.
To my children that keep me going every day :
Rayhanah, Yasmine, Yusuf, Ayoub, Sulaiman, Musa and Mariam.
To my kindred spirit, Almanfaluthi,
who has always been a constant support and joy in my life.

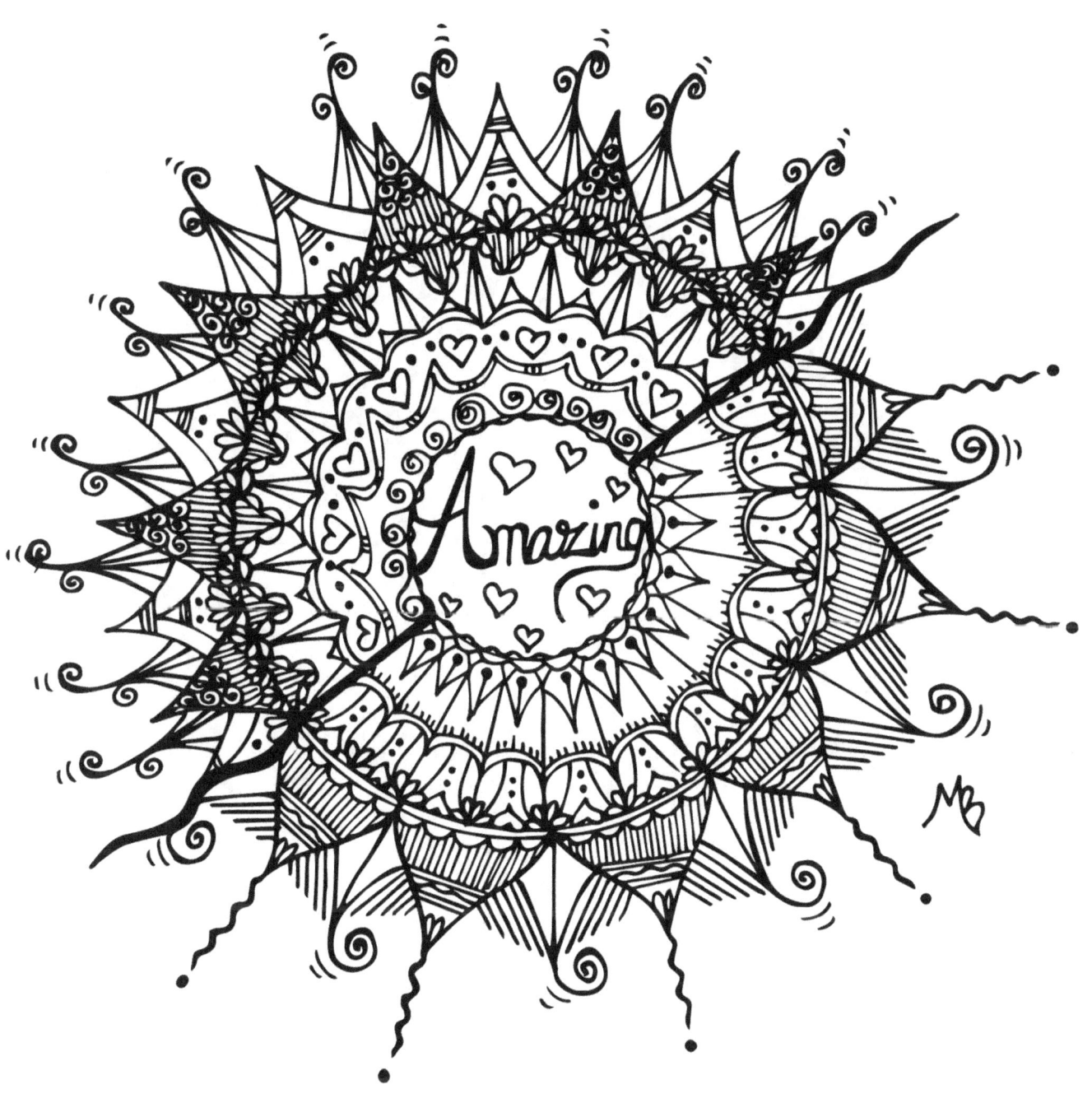

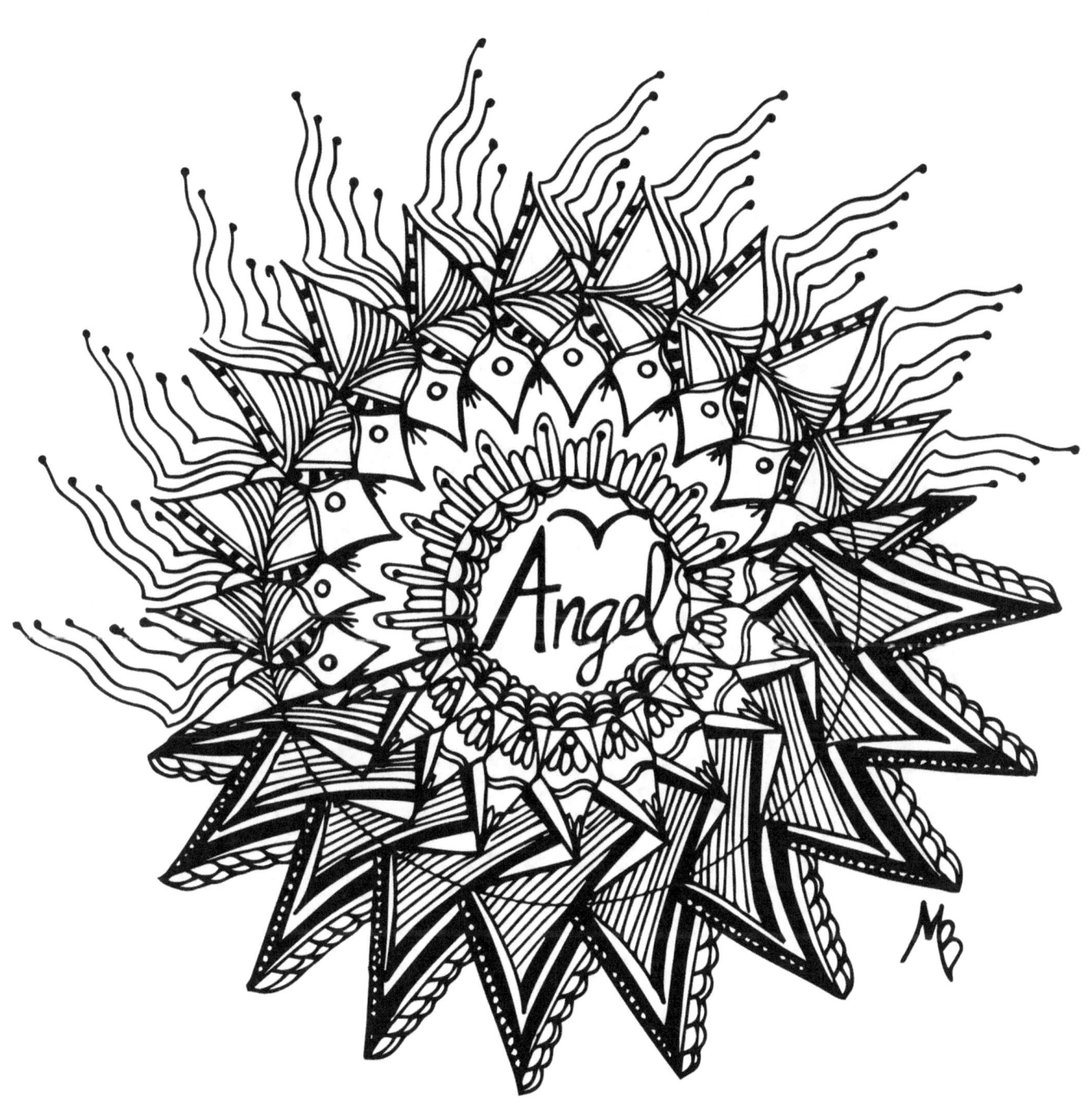

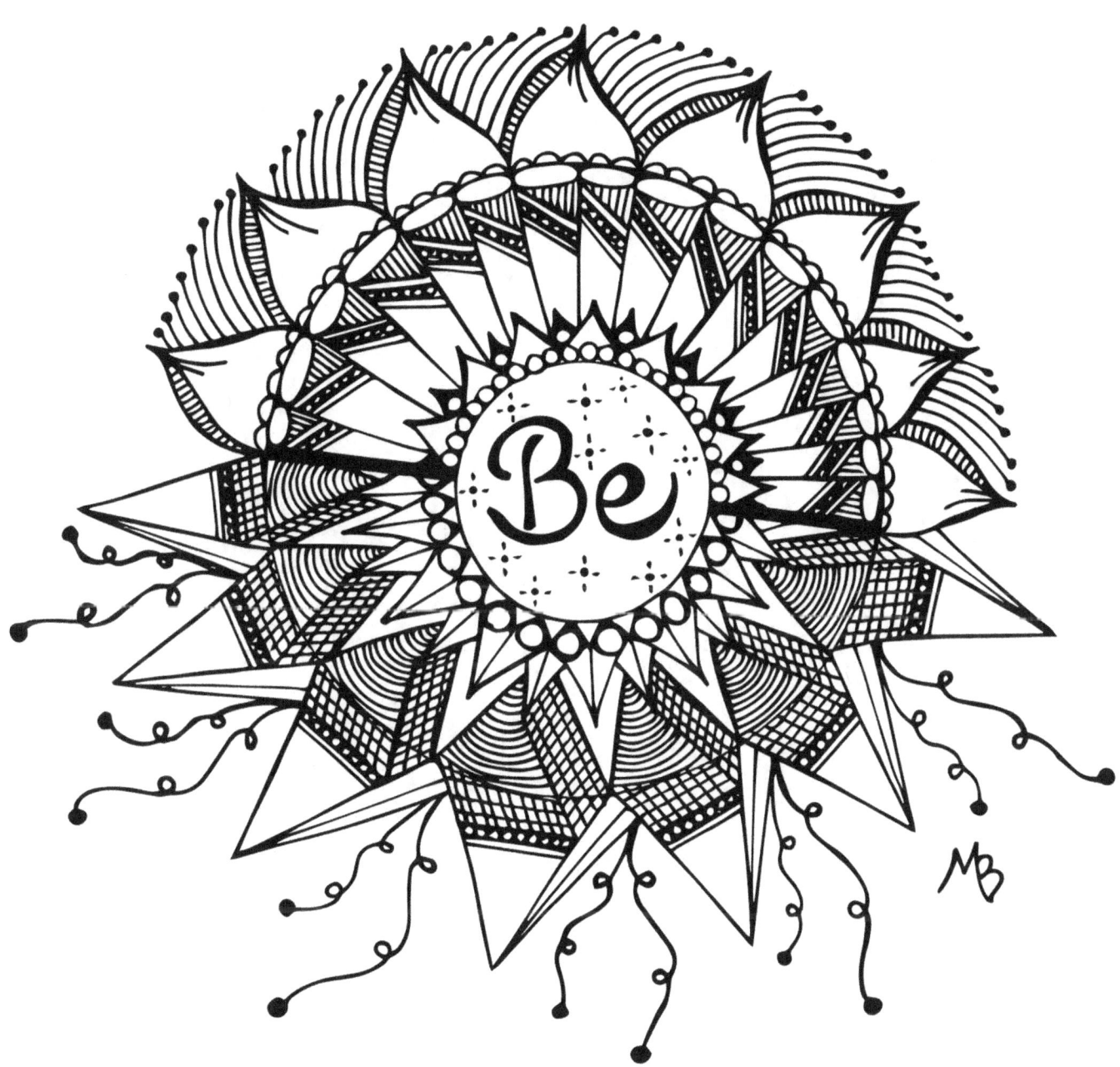

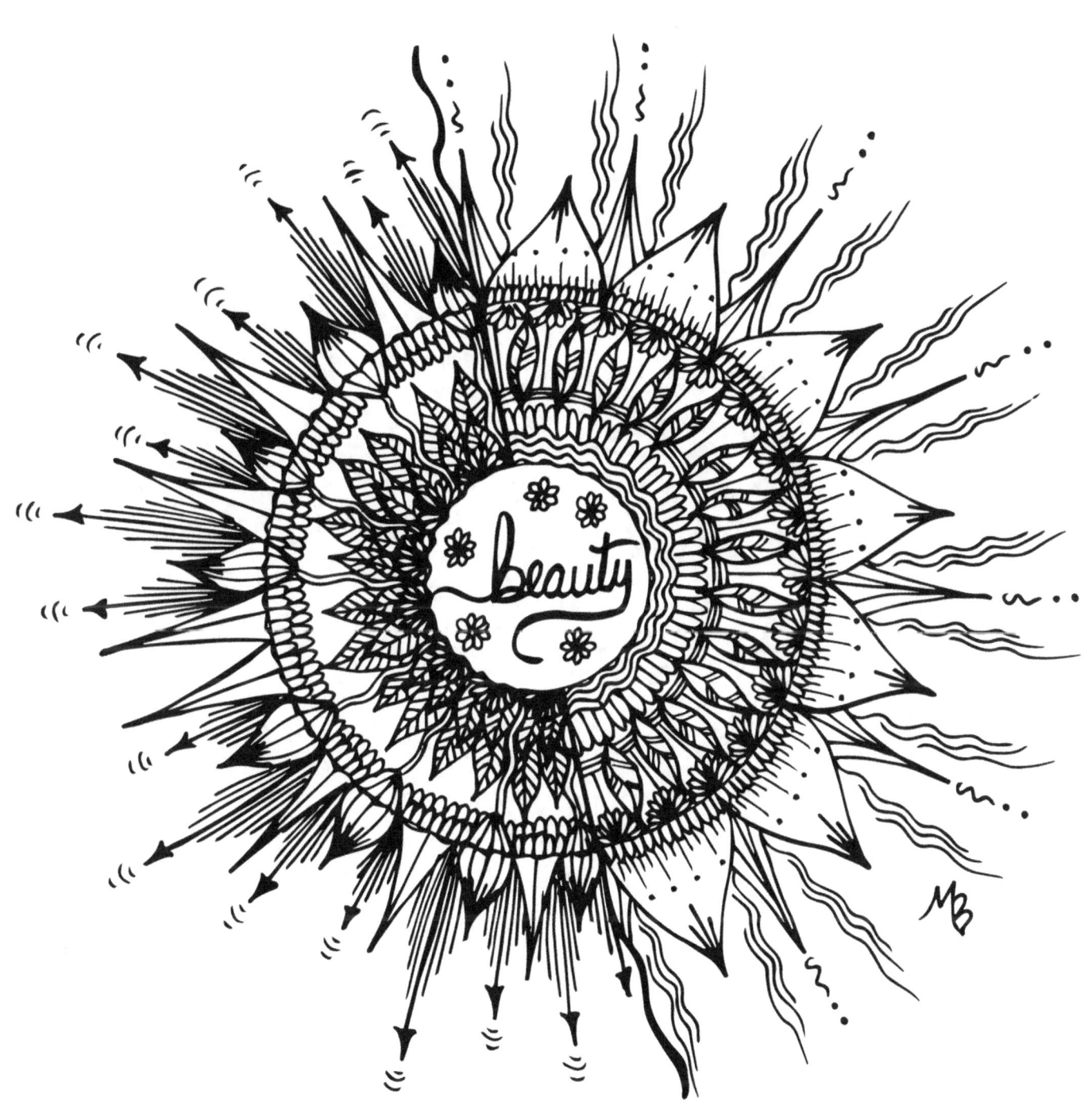

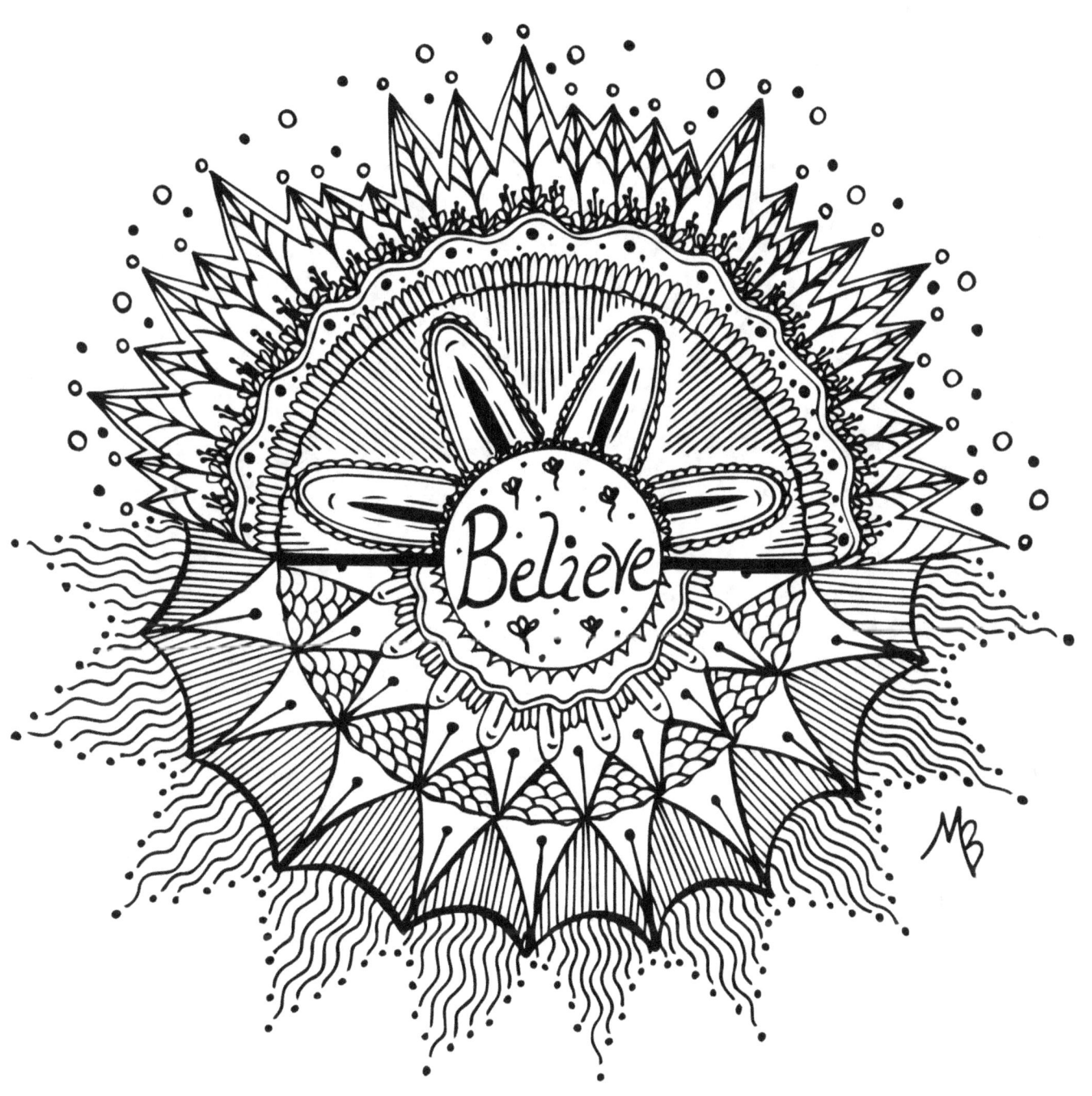

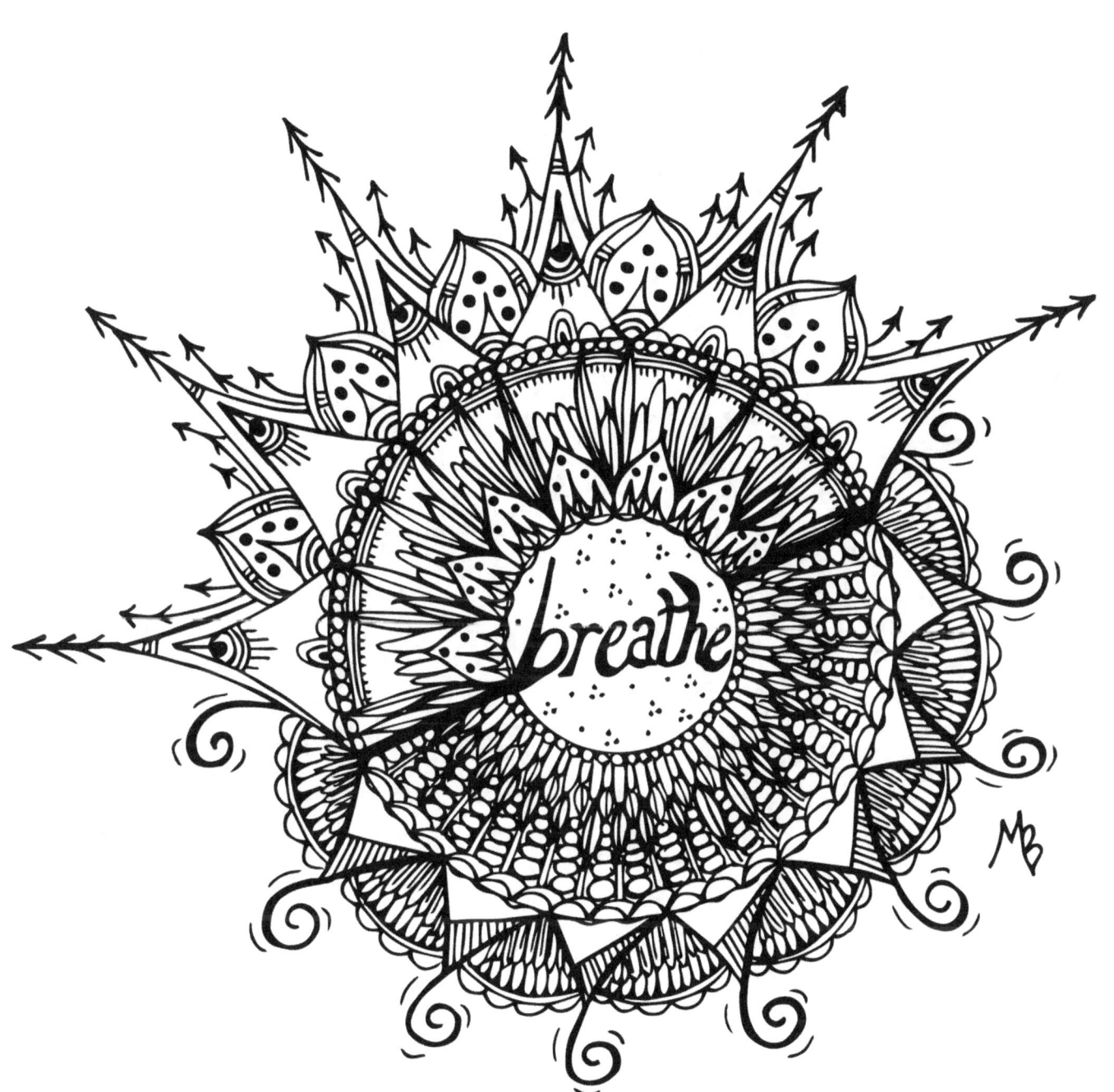

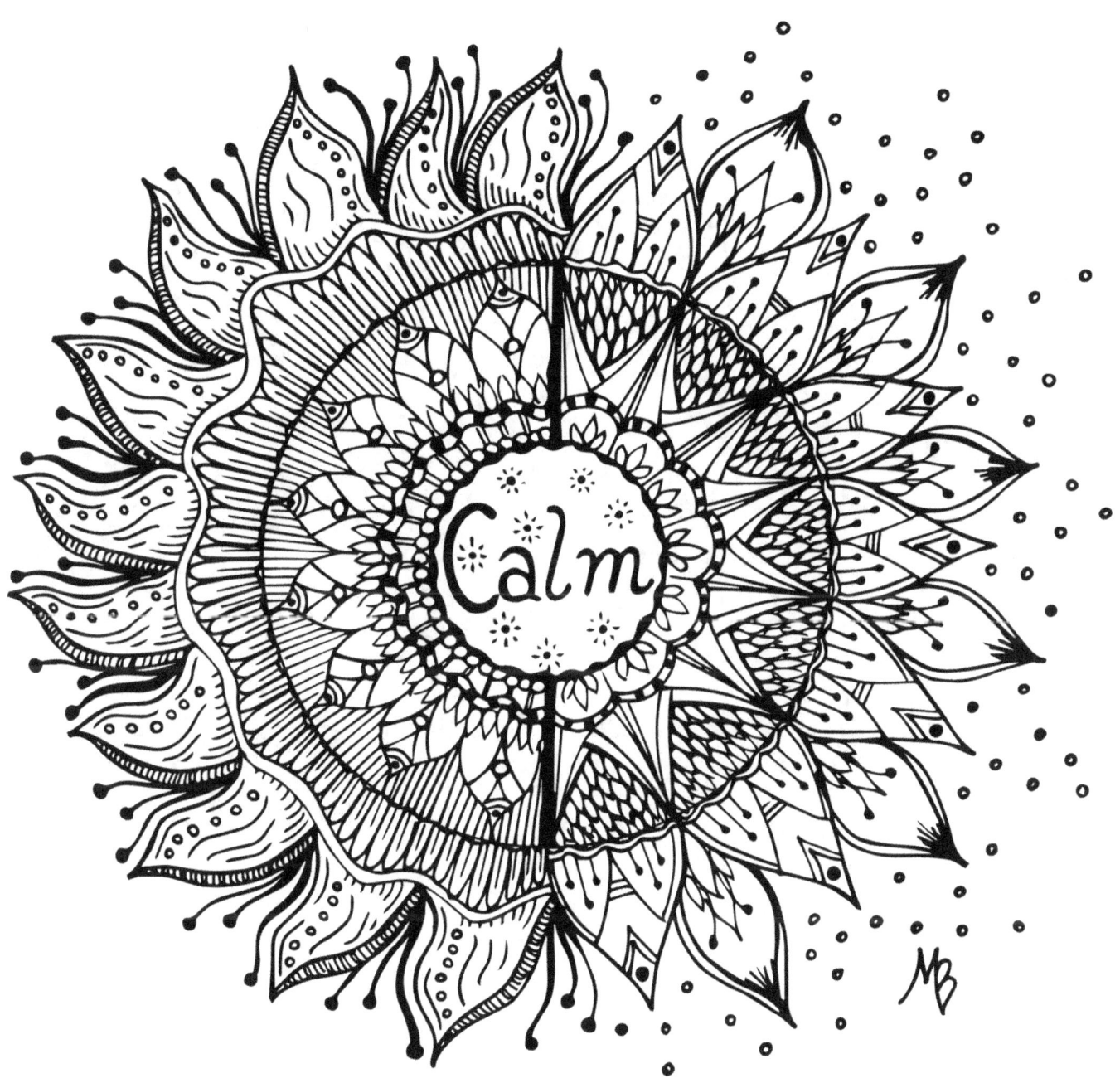

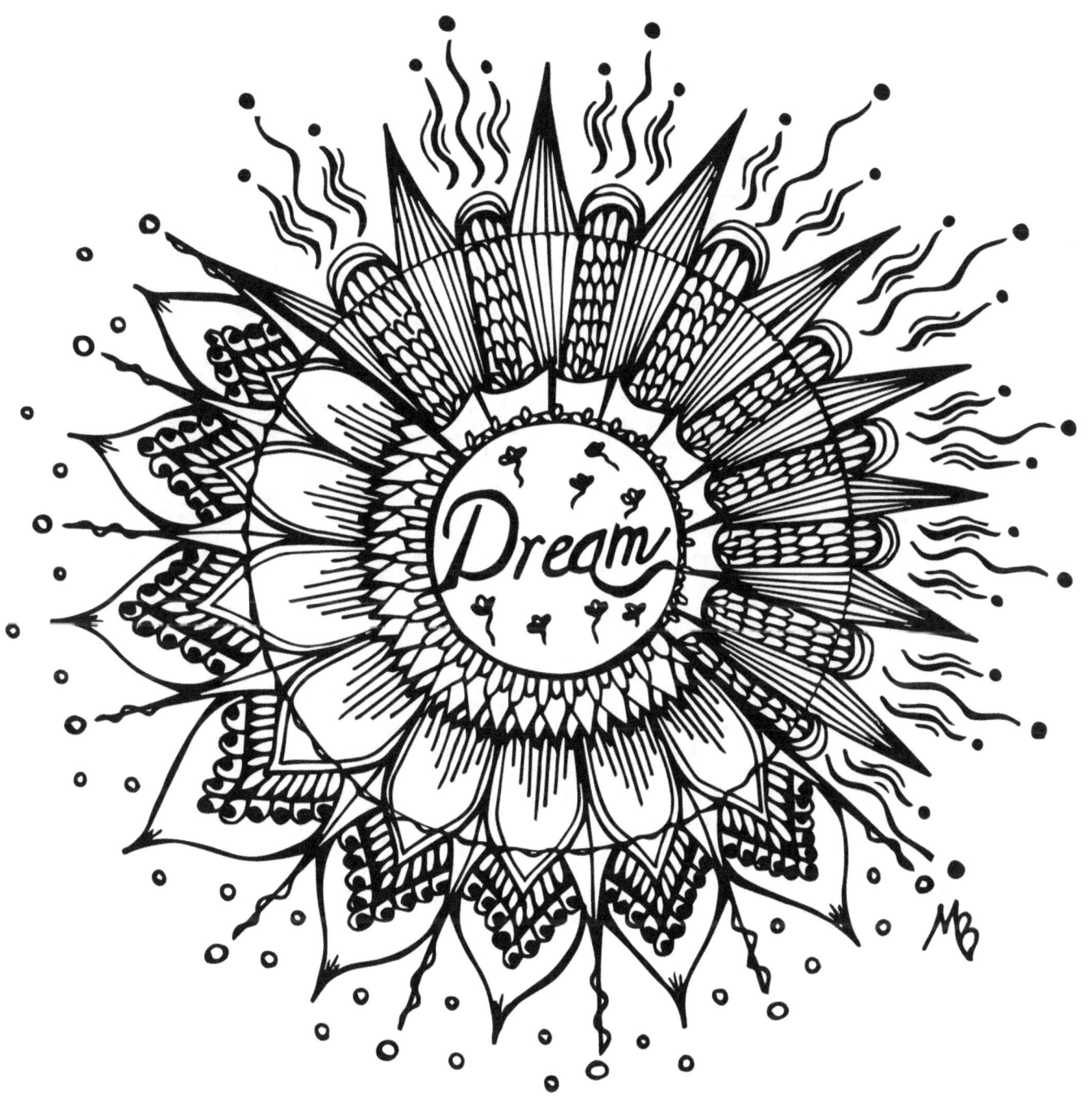

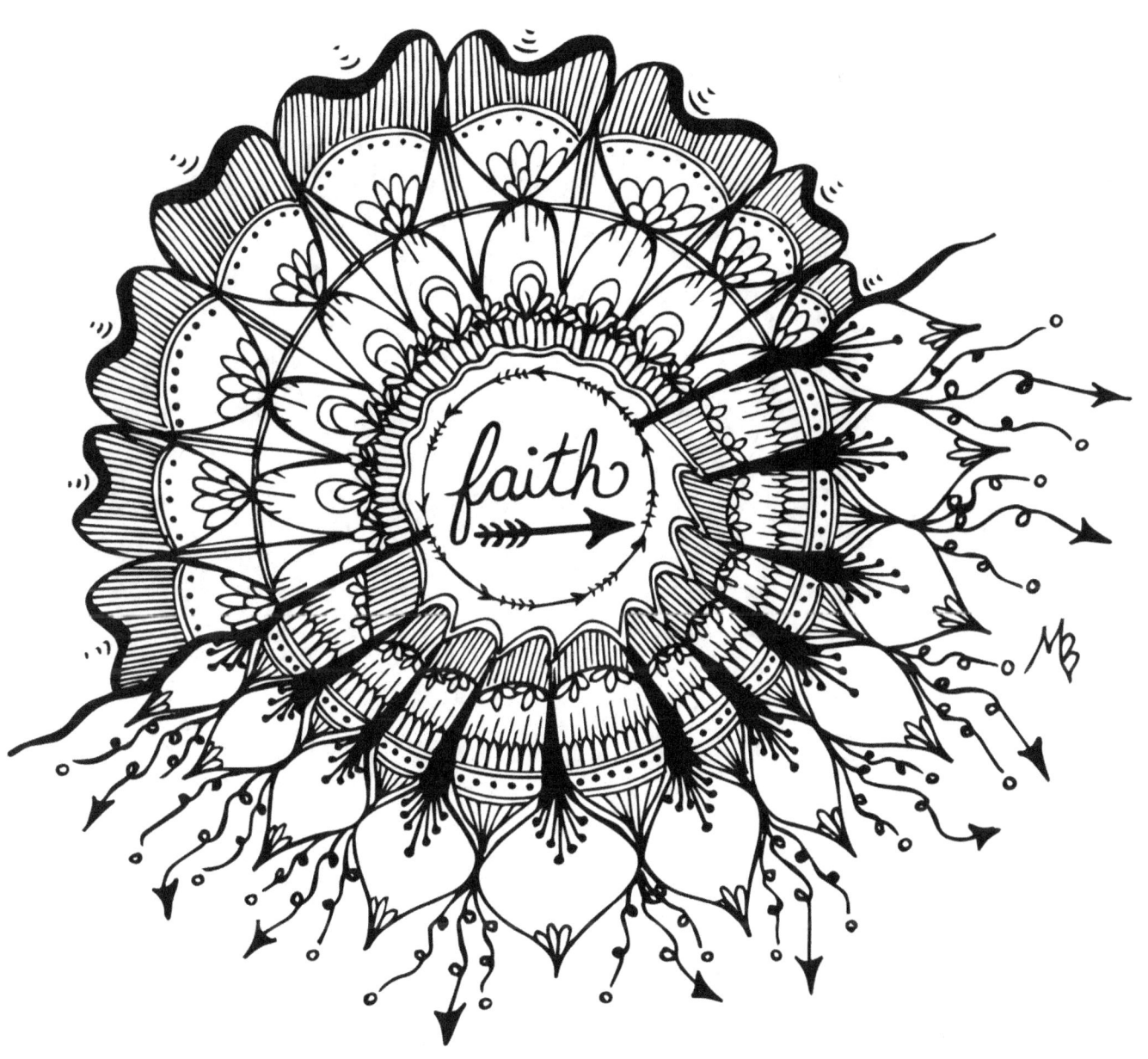

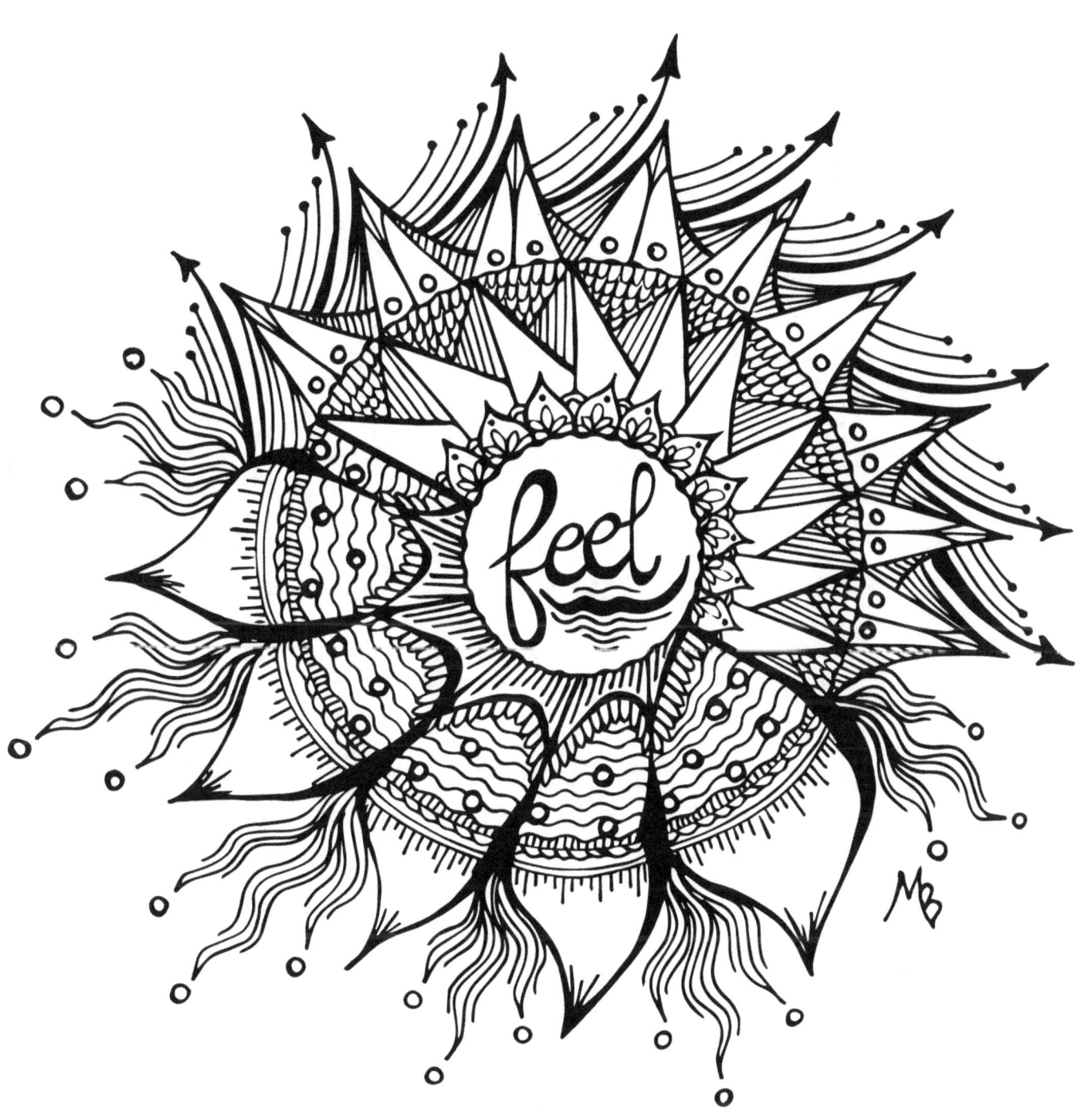

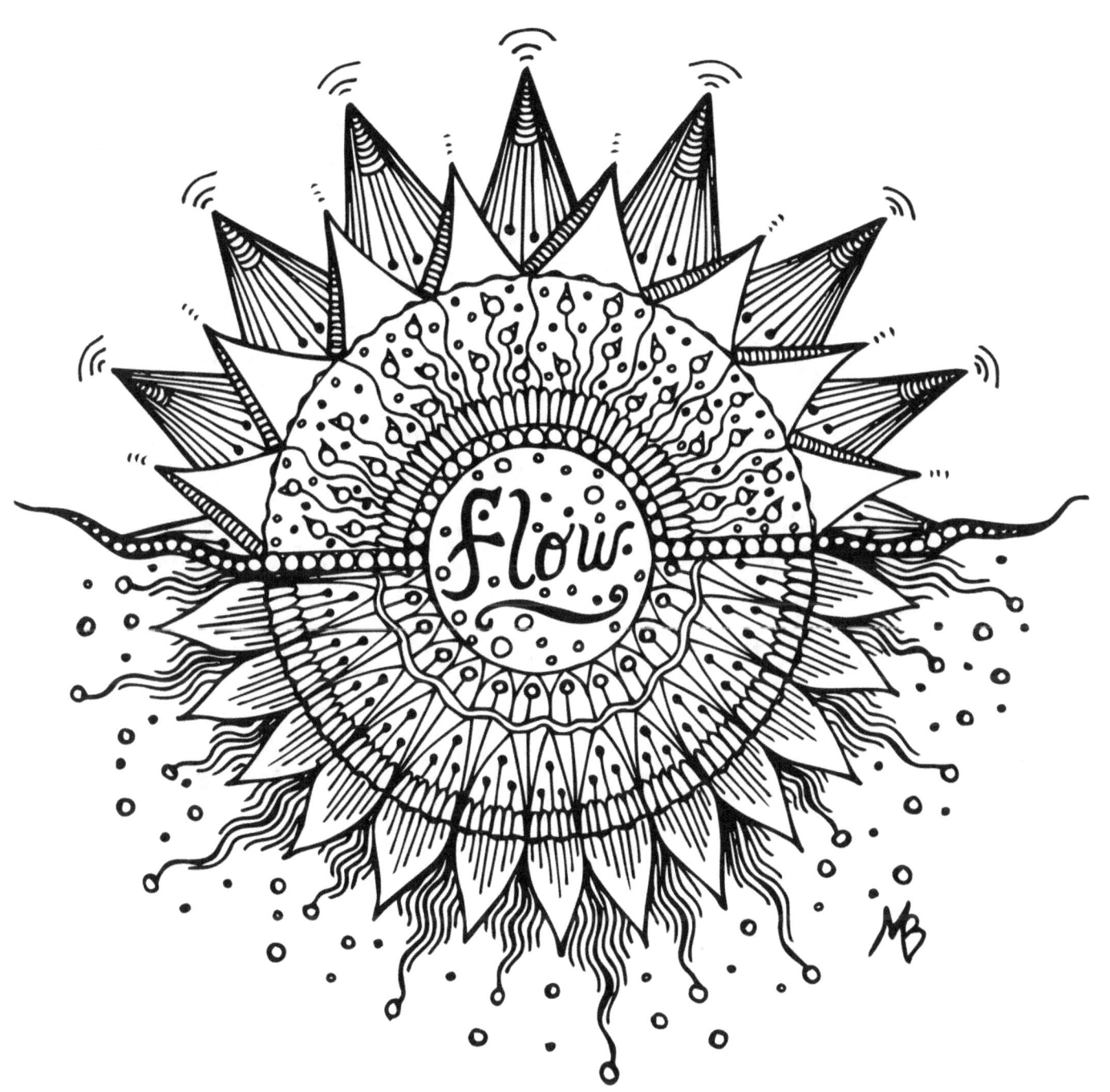

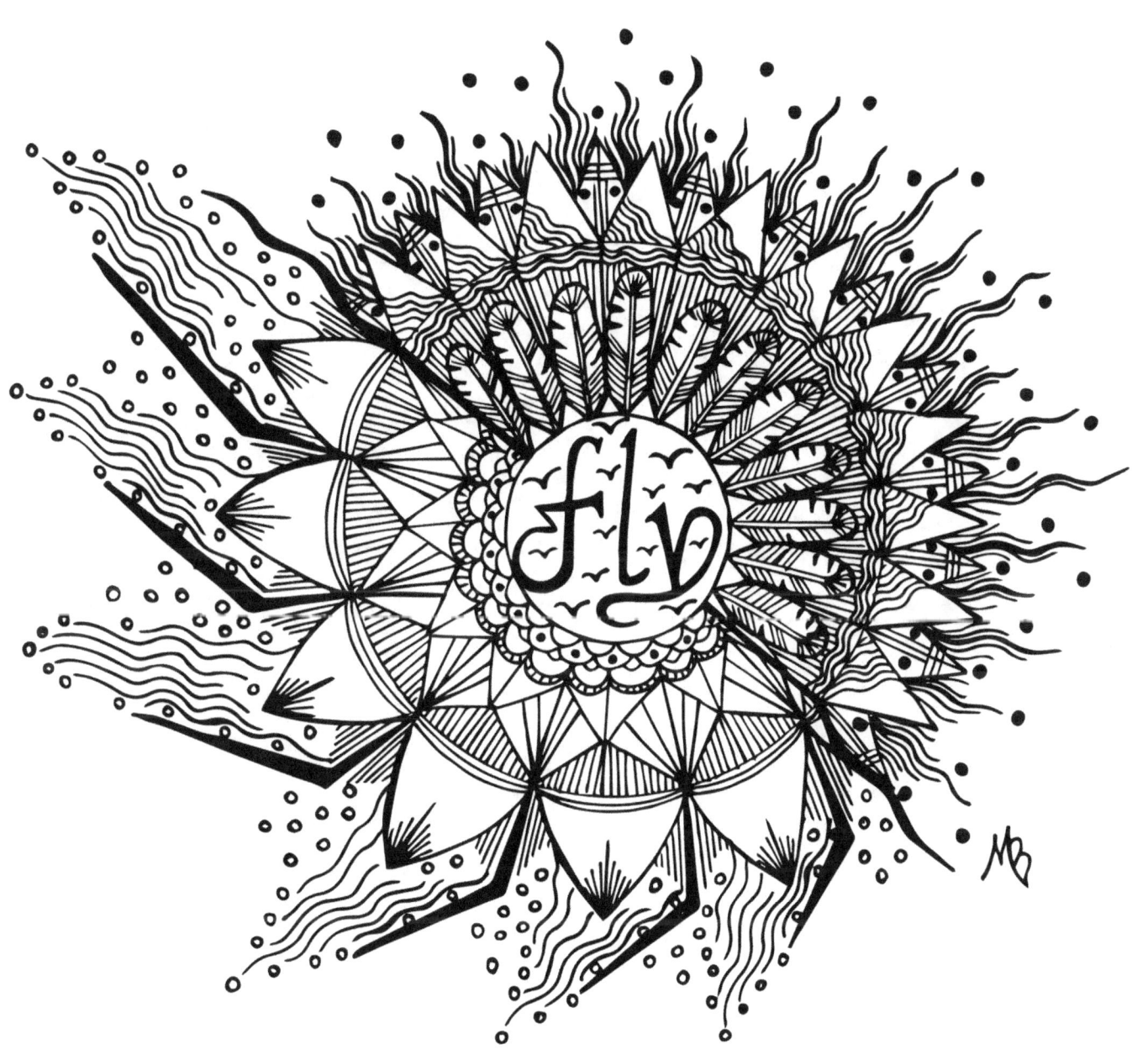

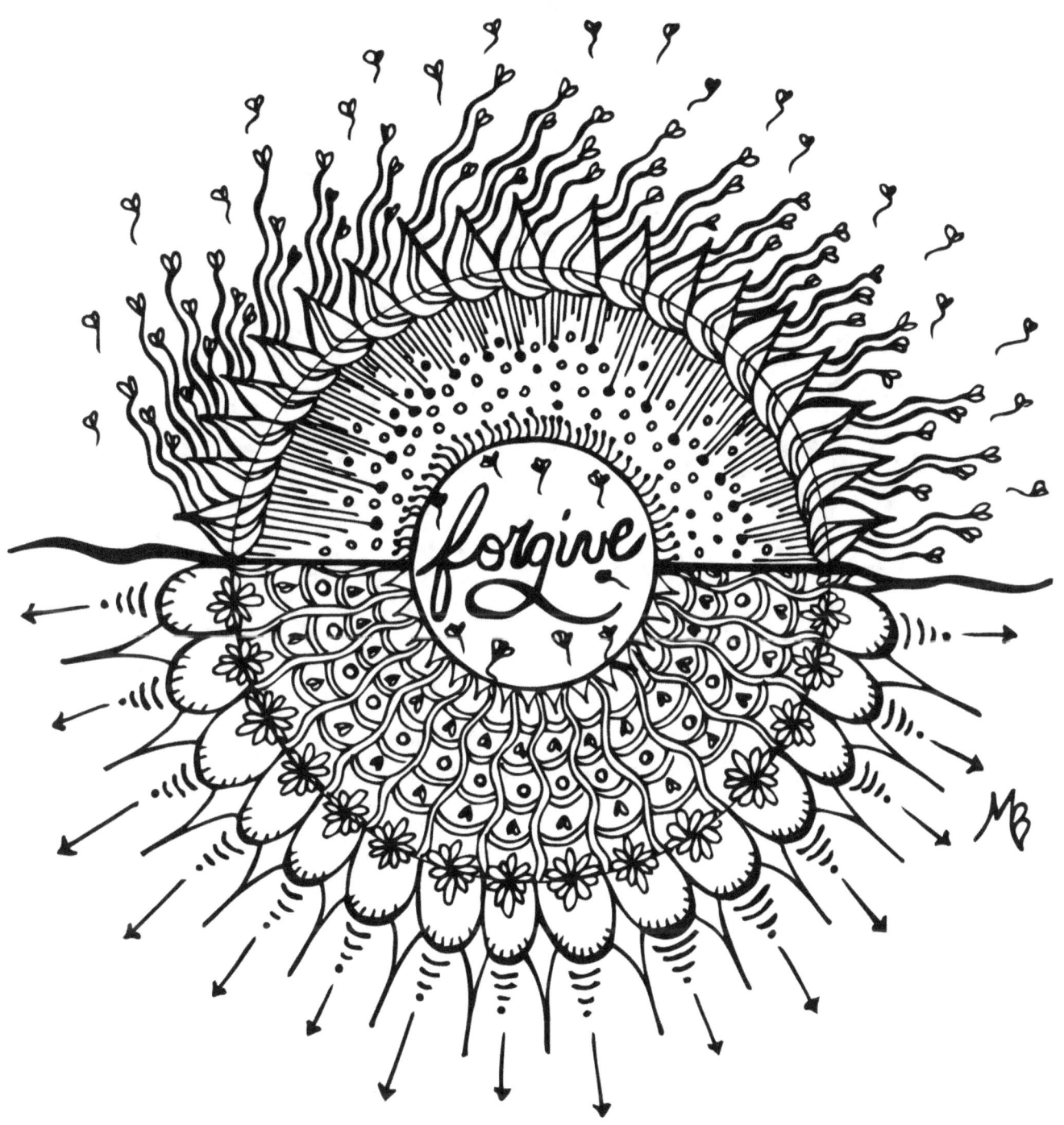

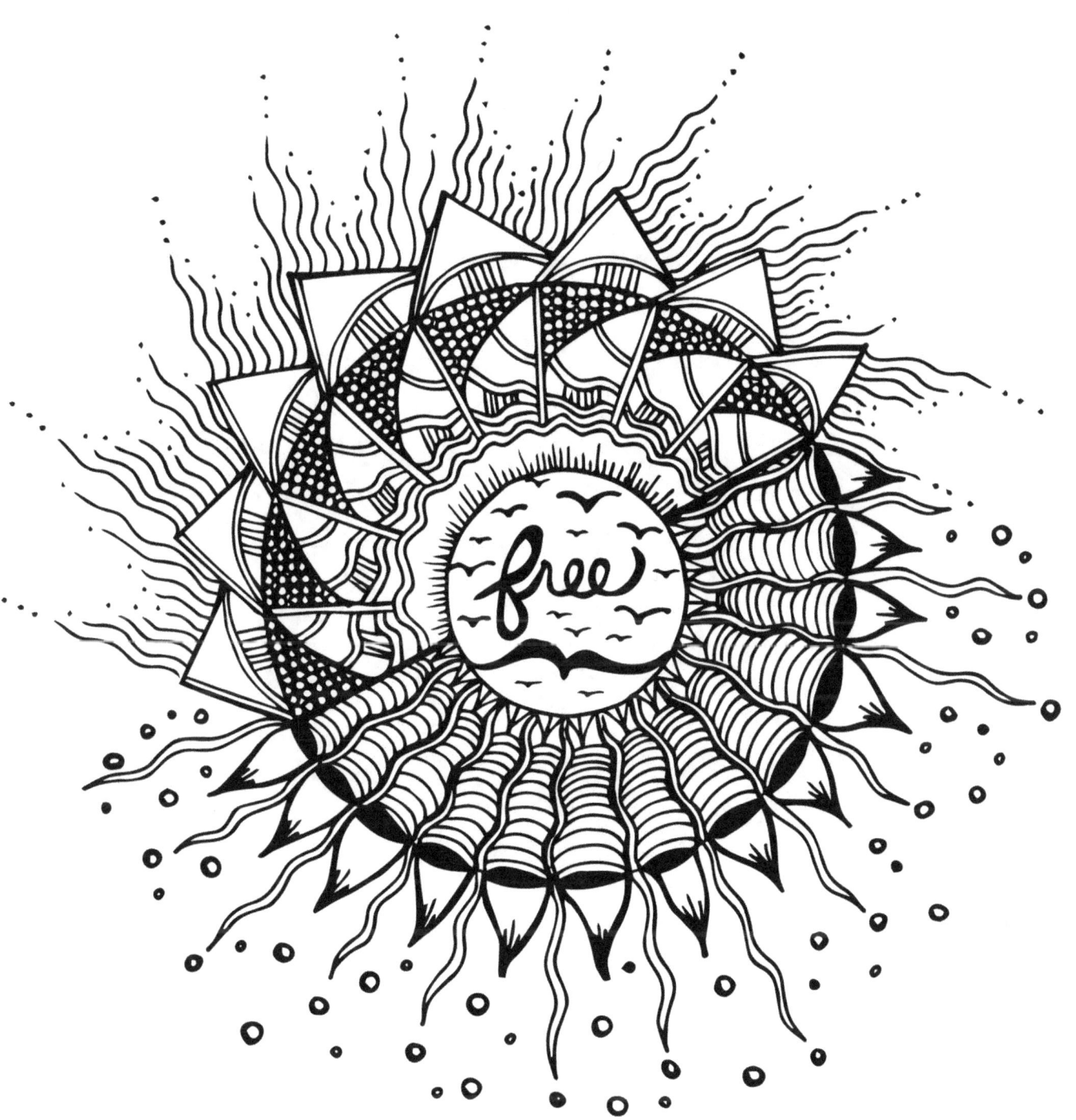

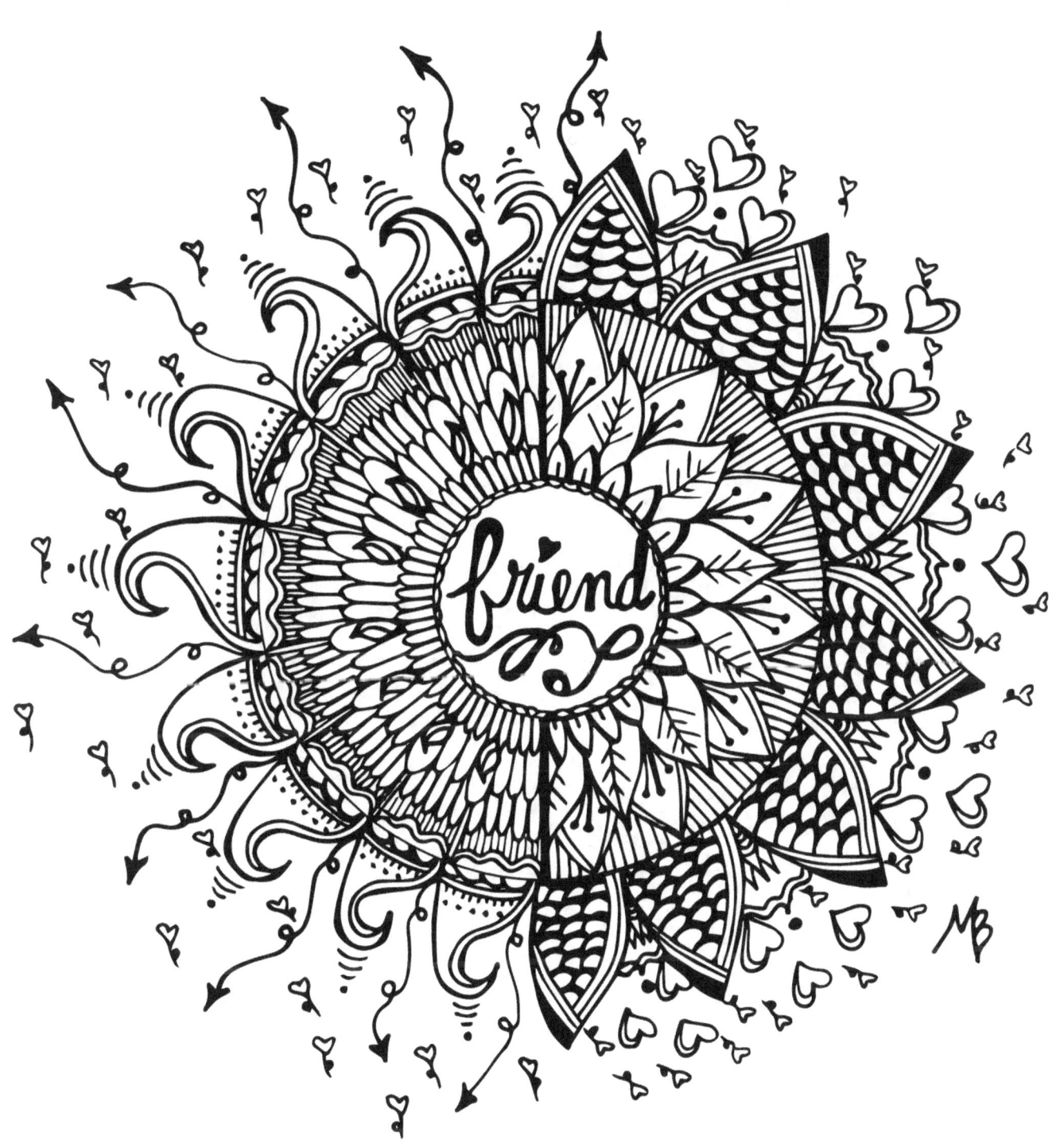

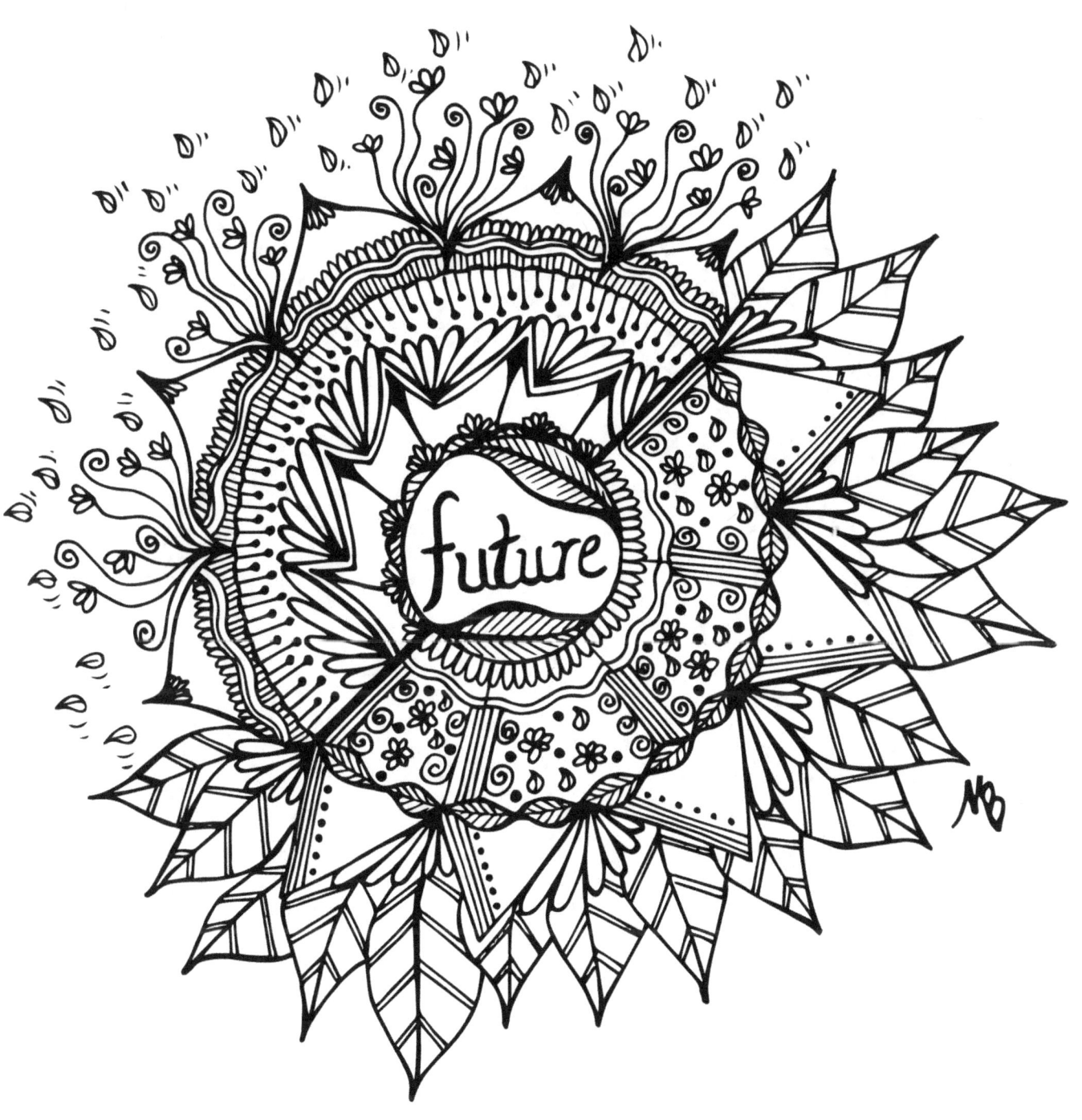

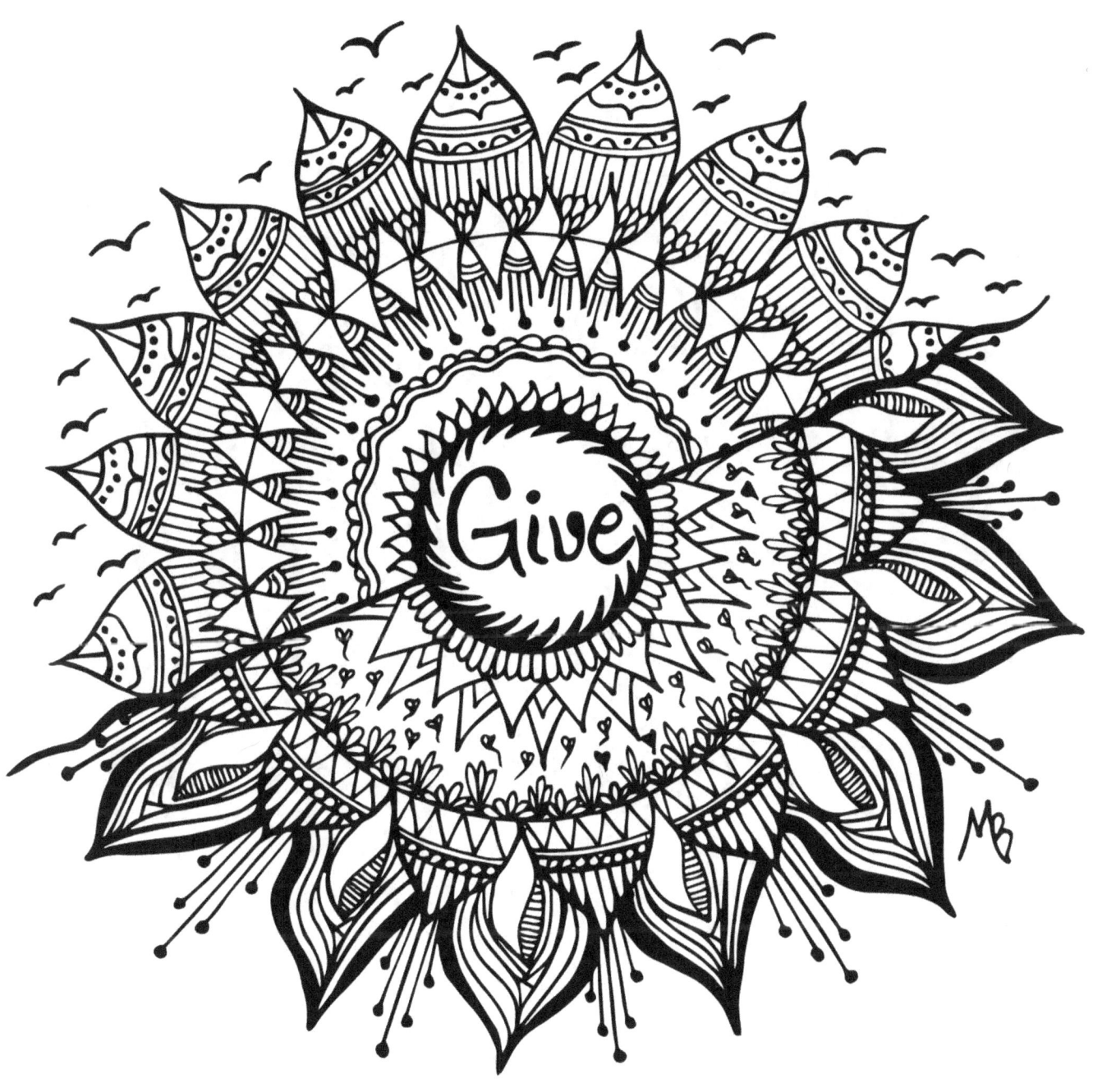

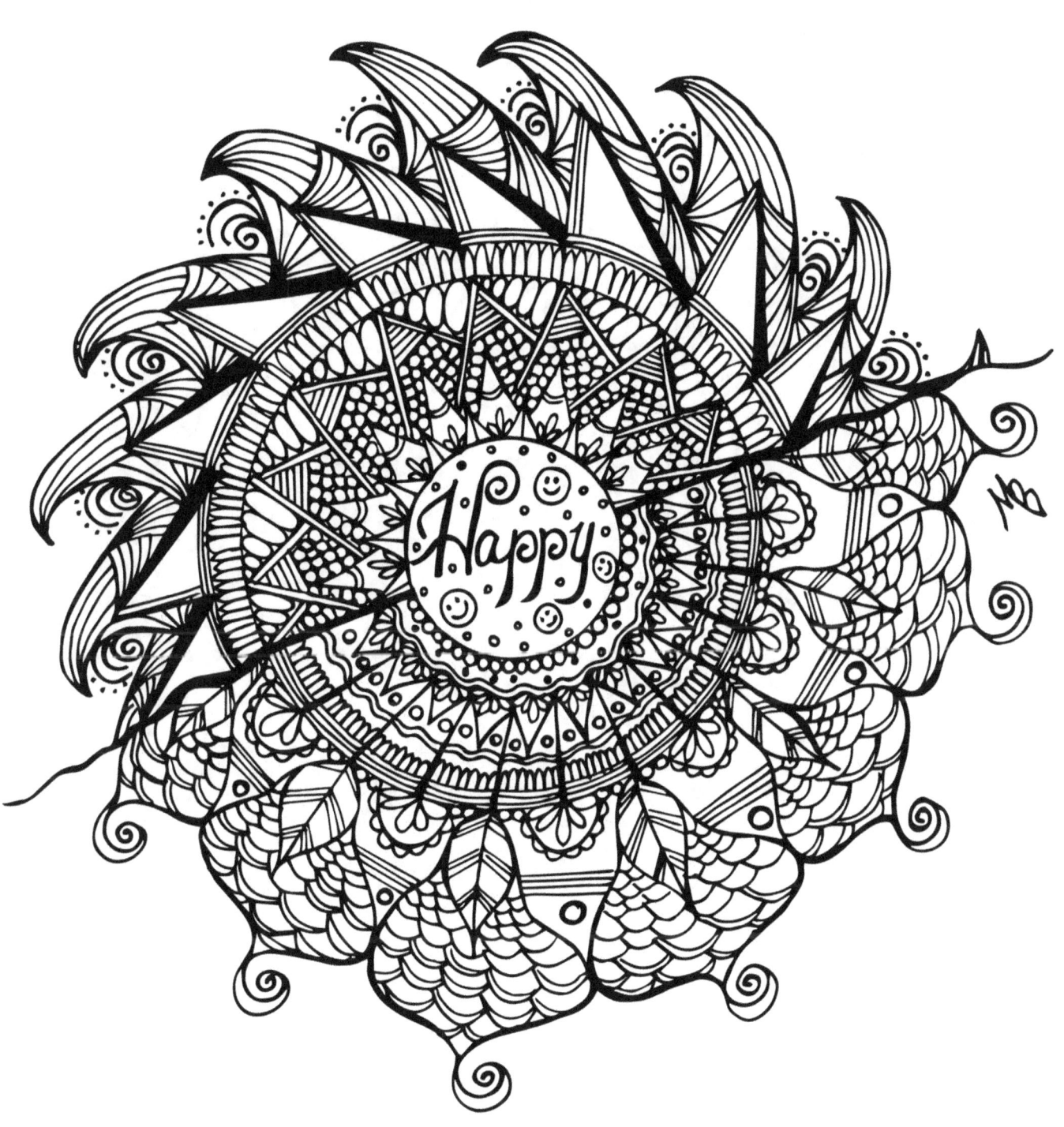

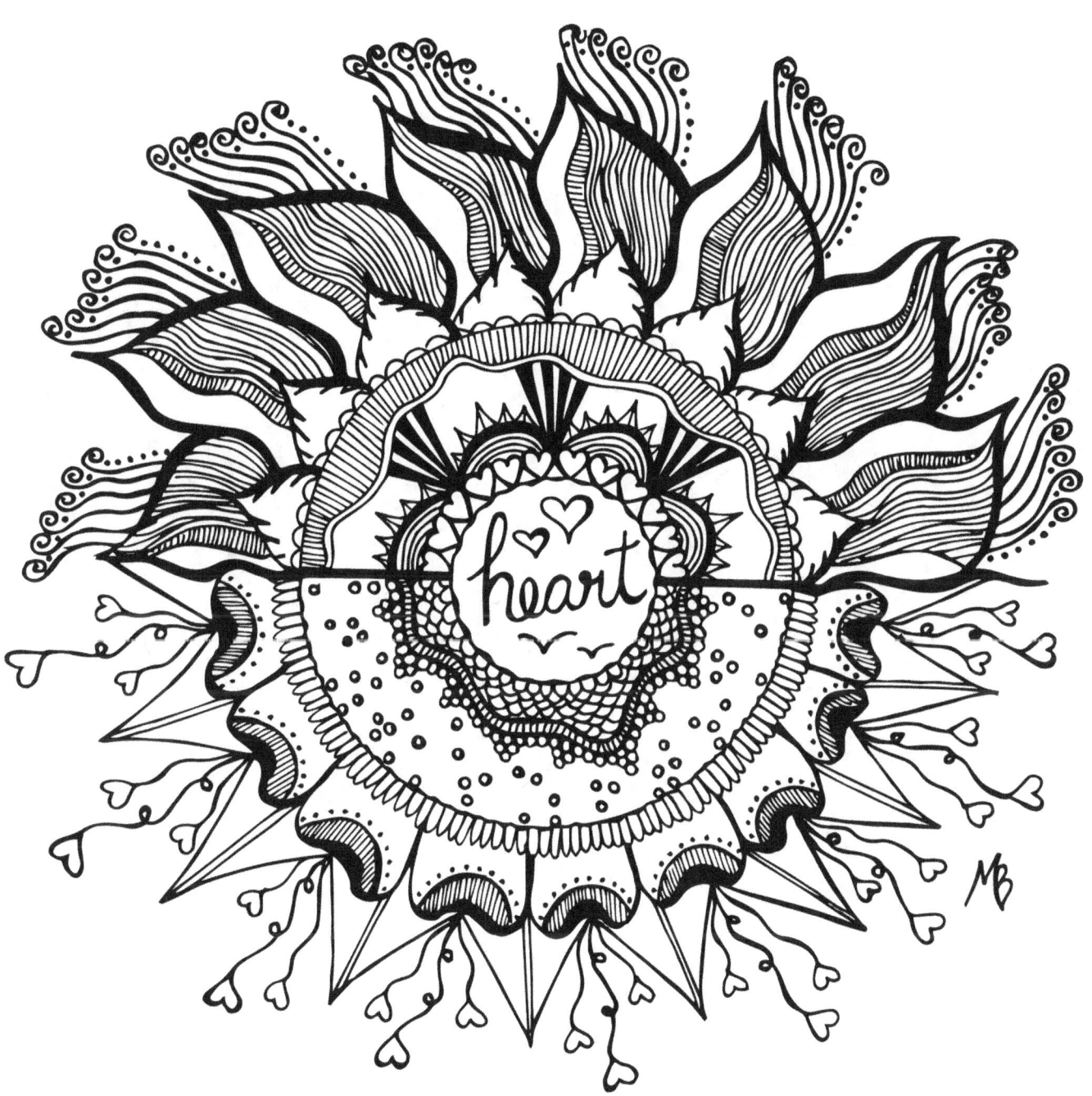

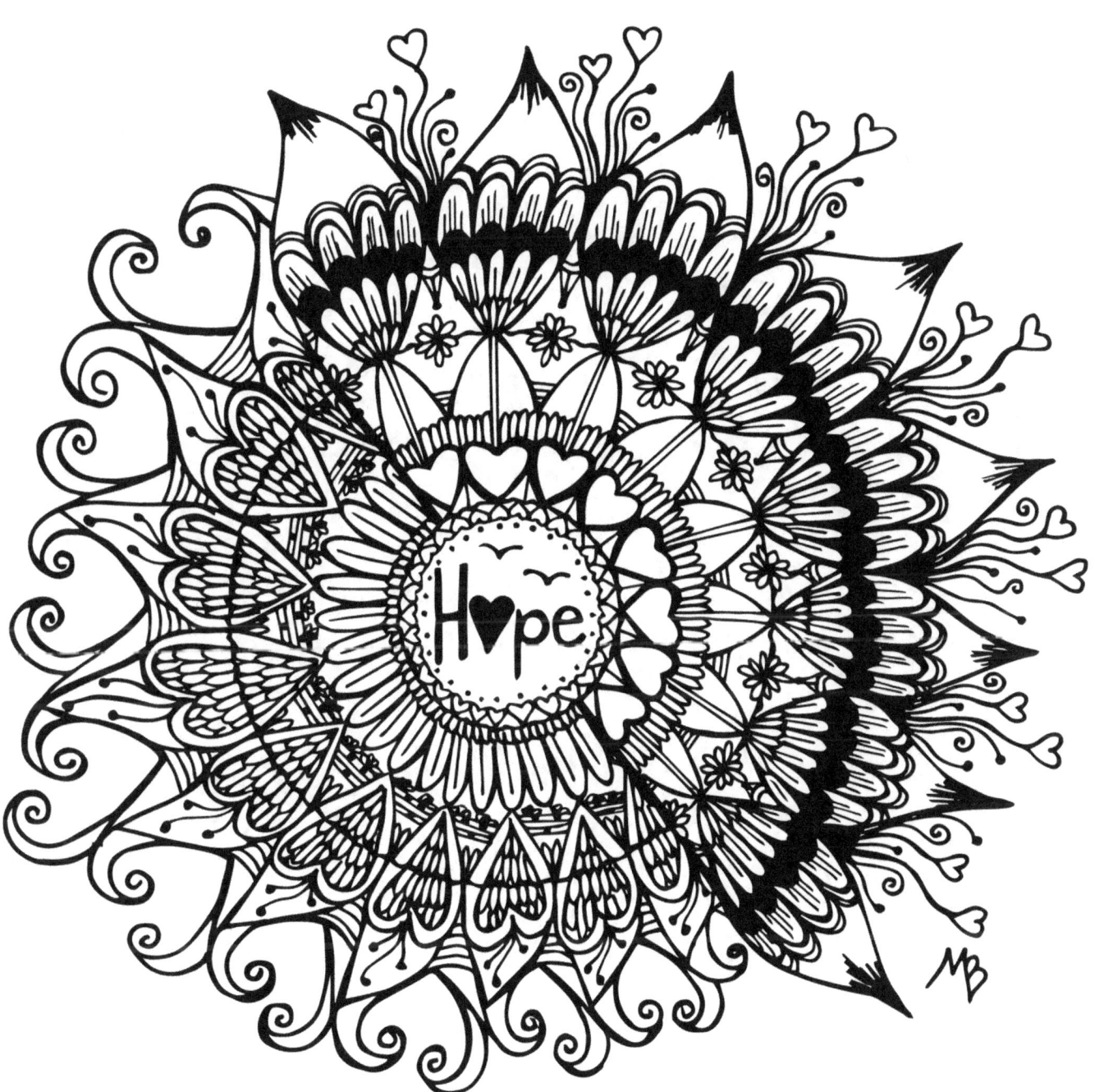

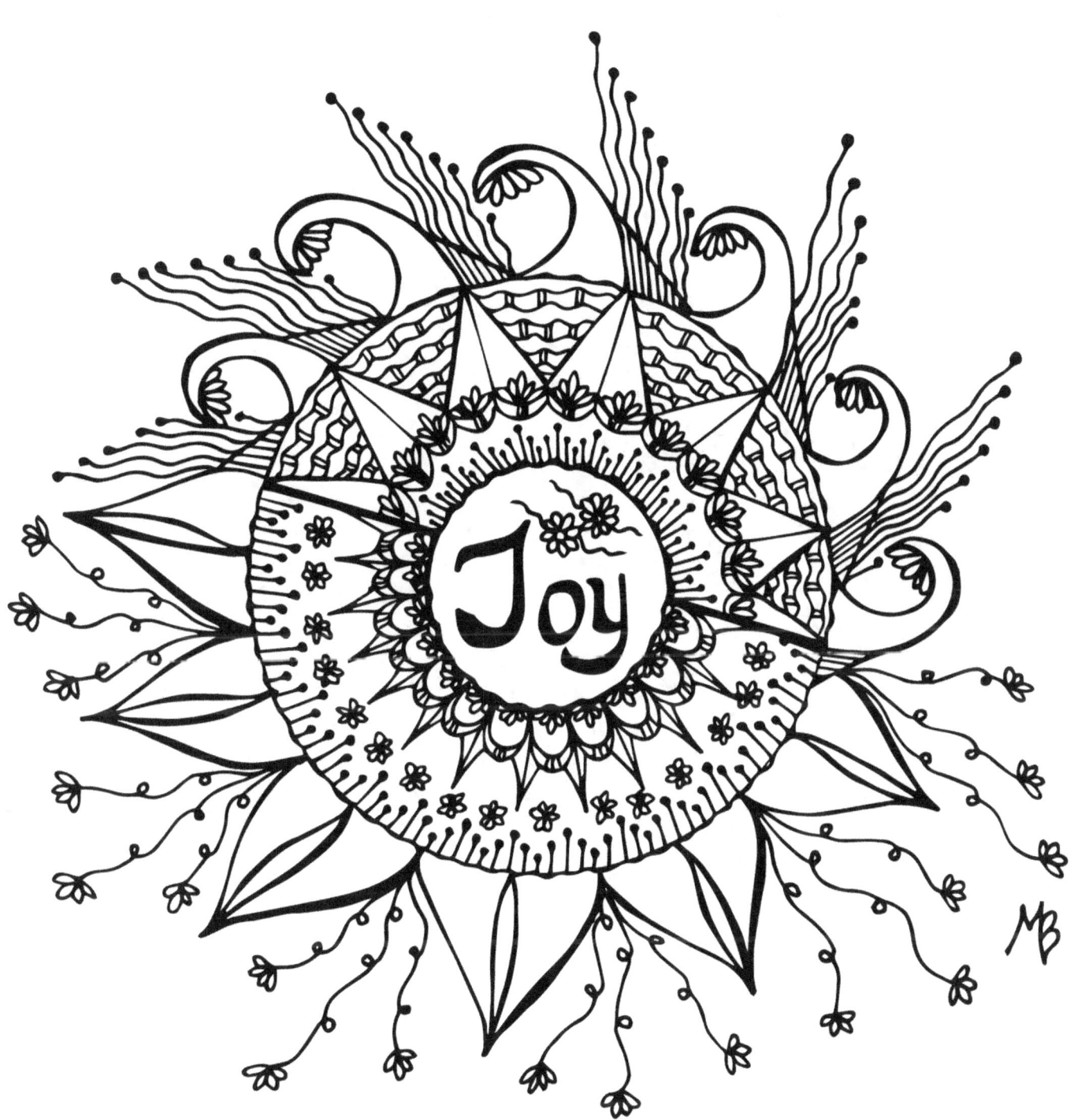

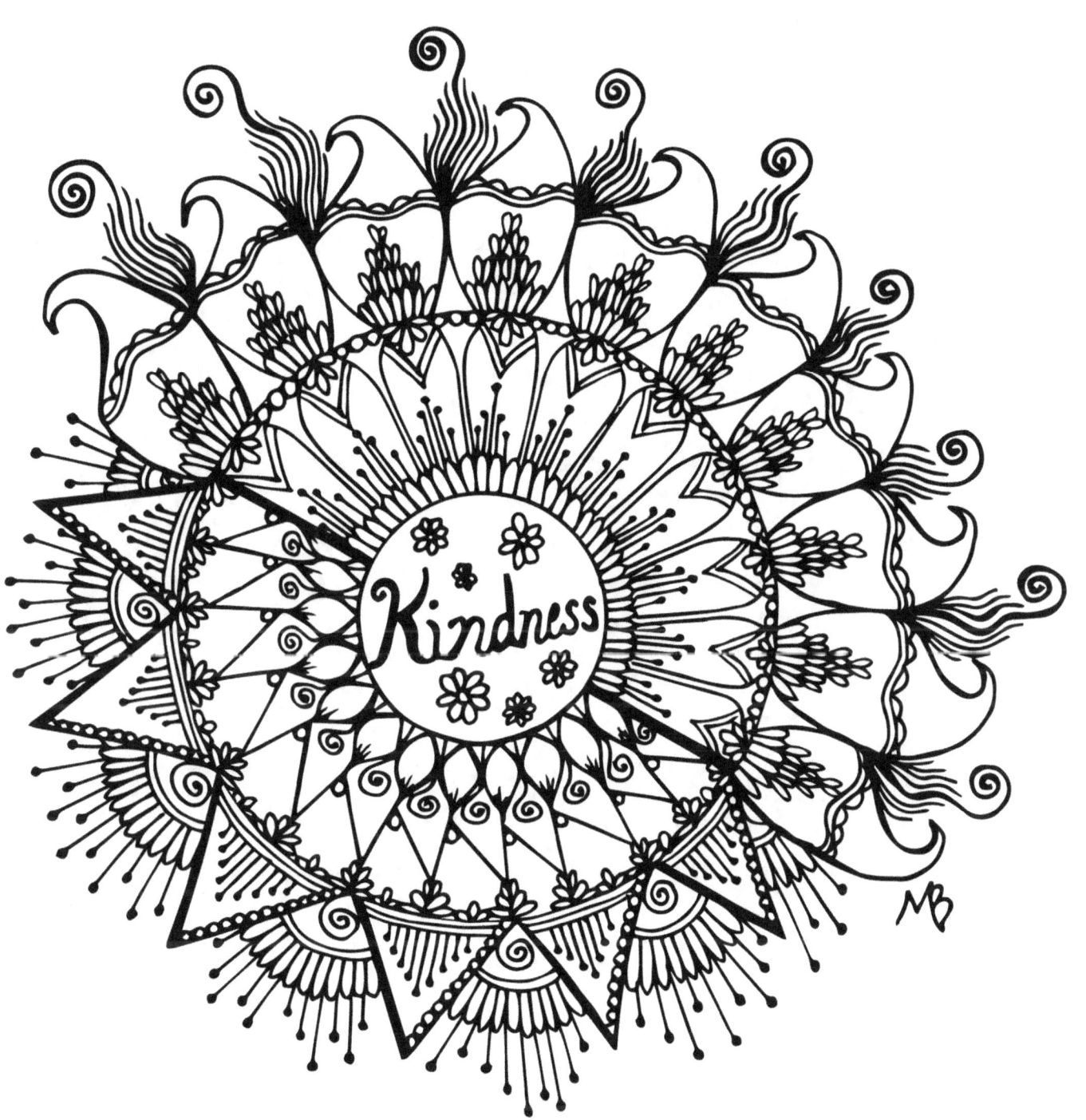

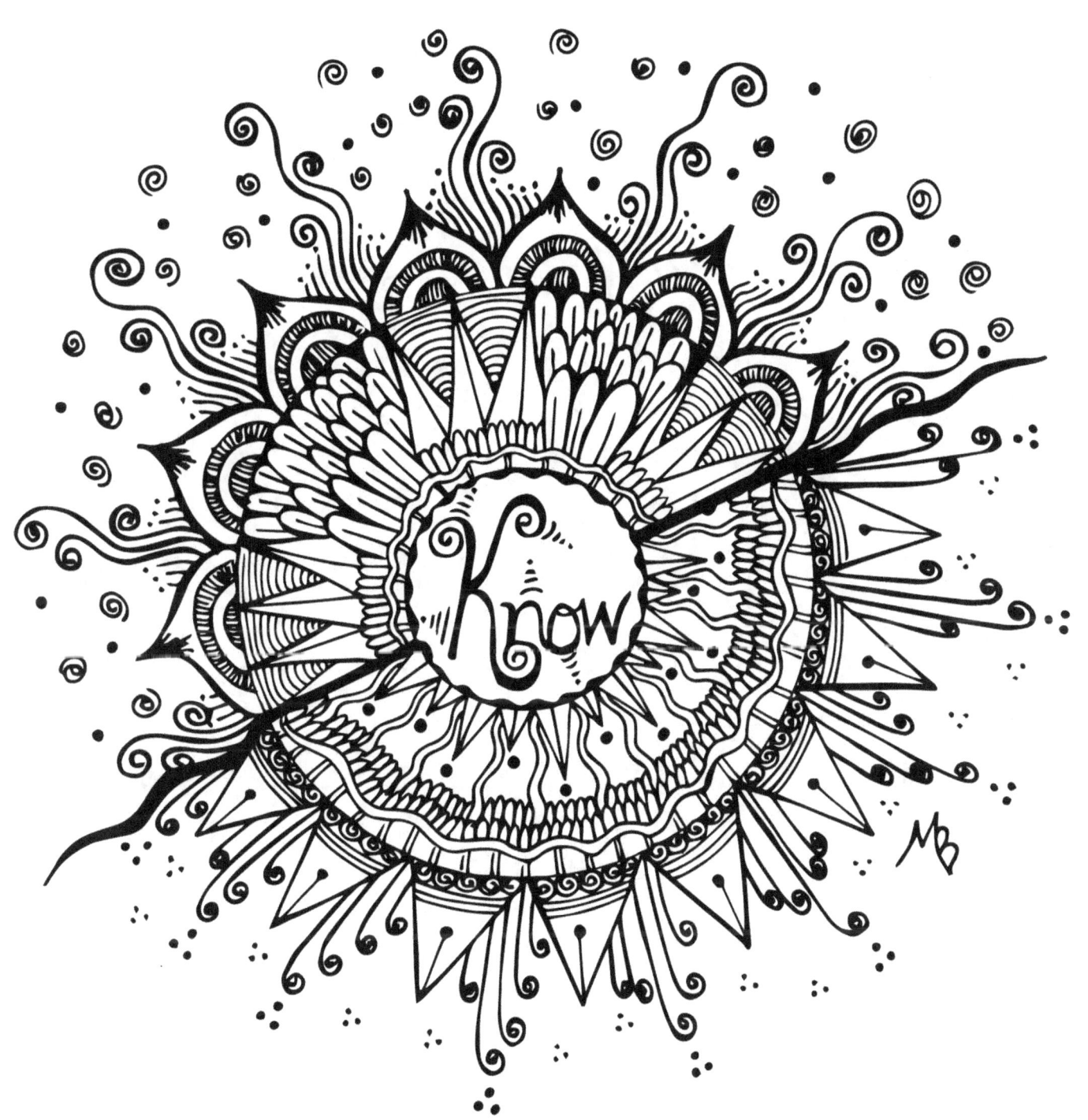

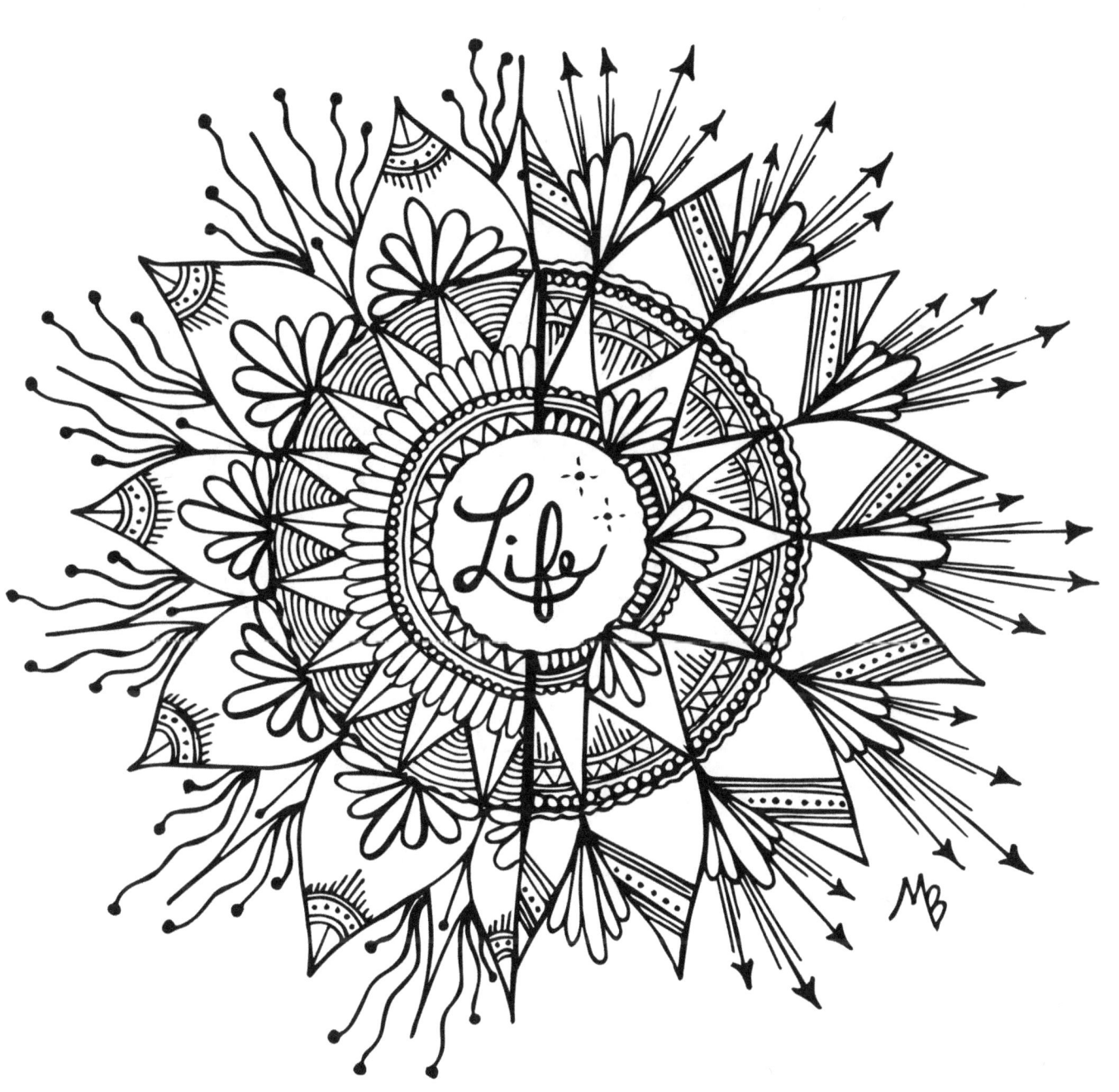

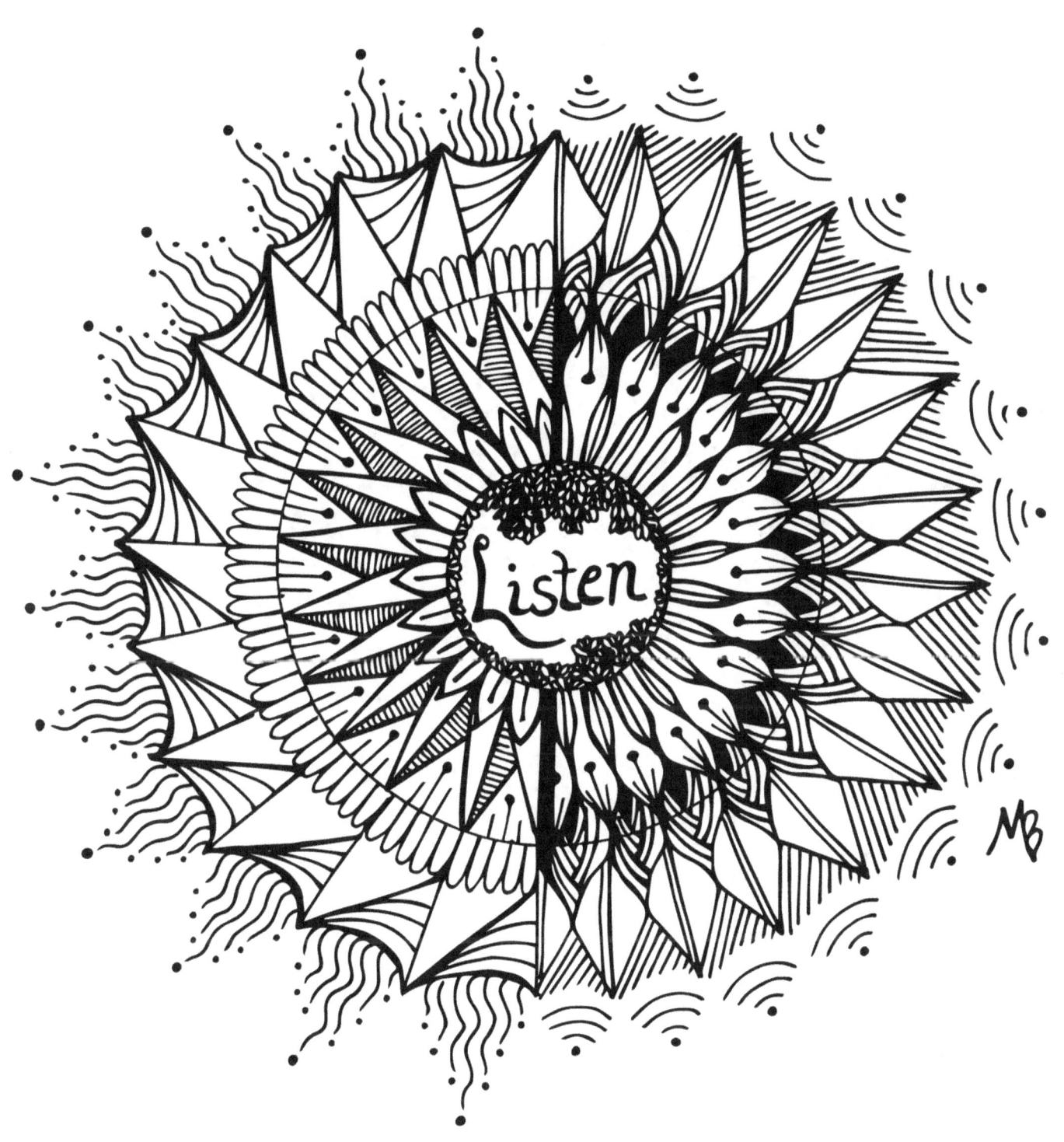

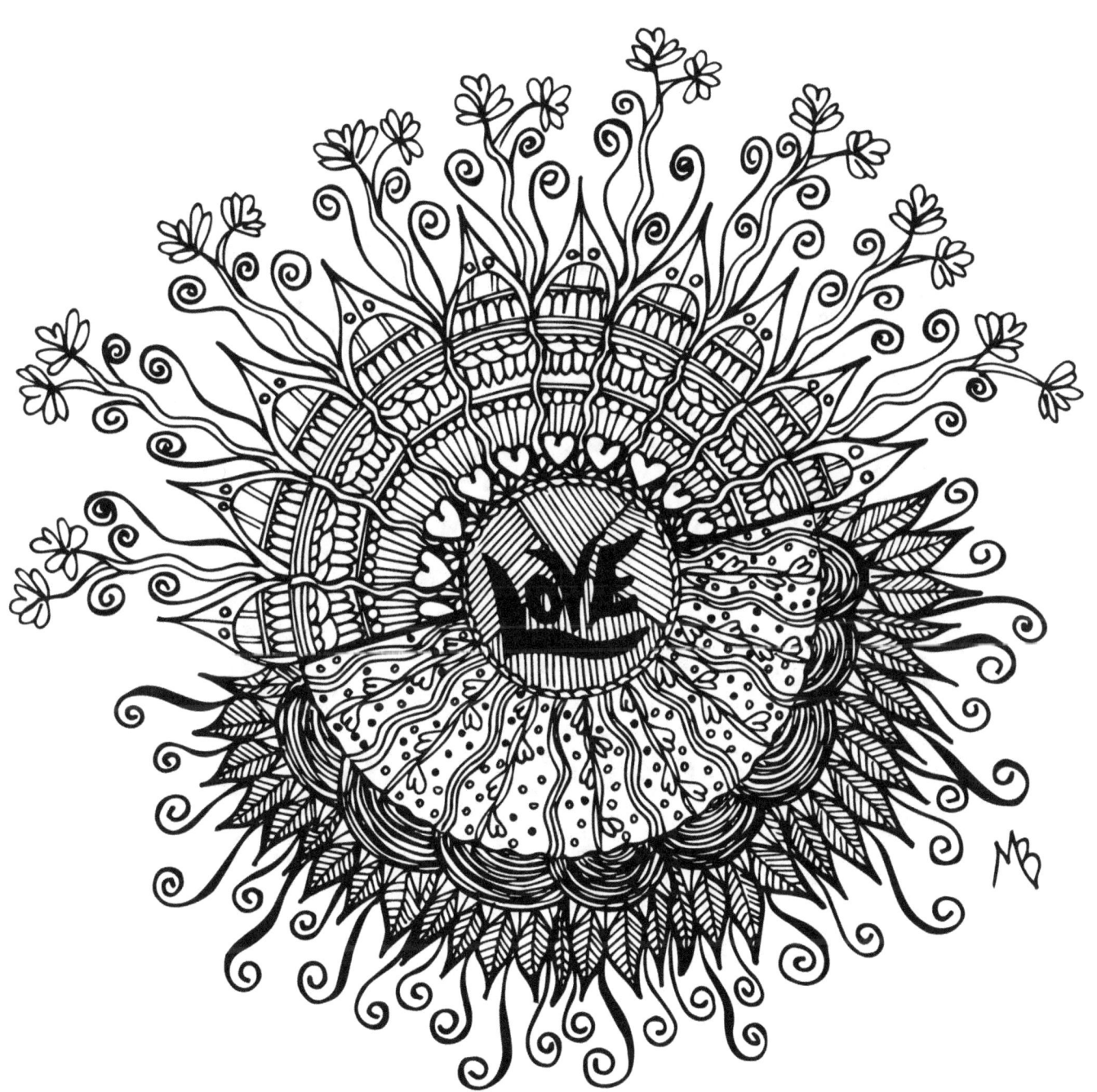

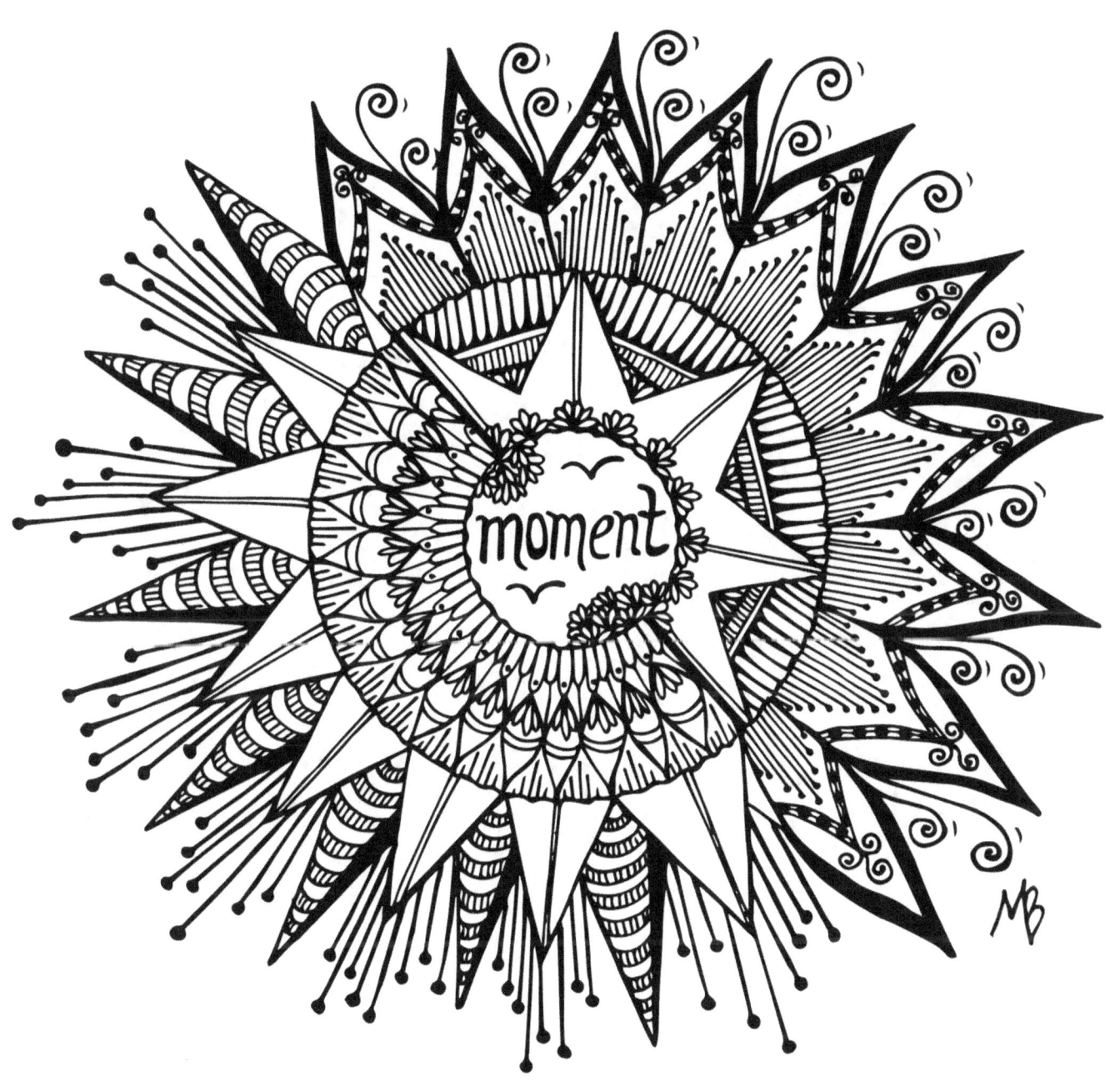

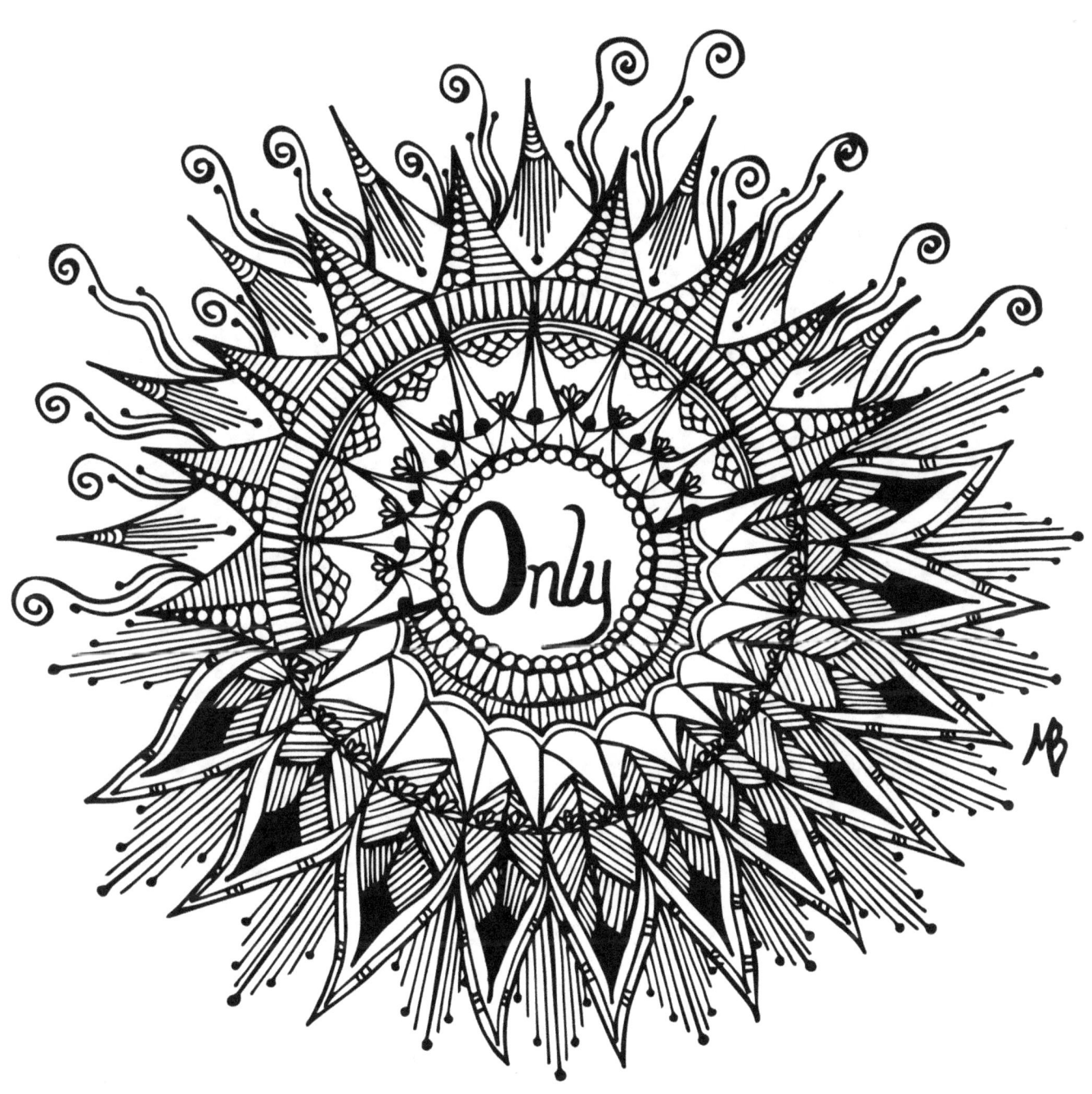

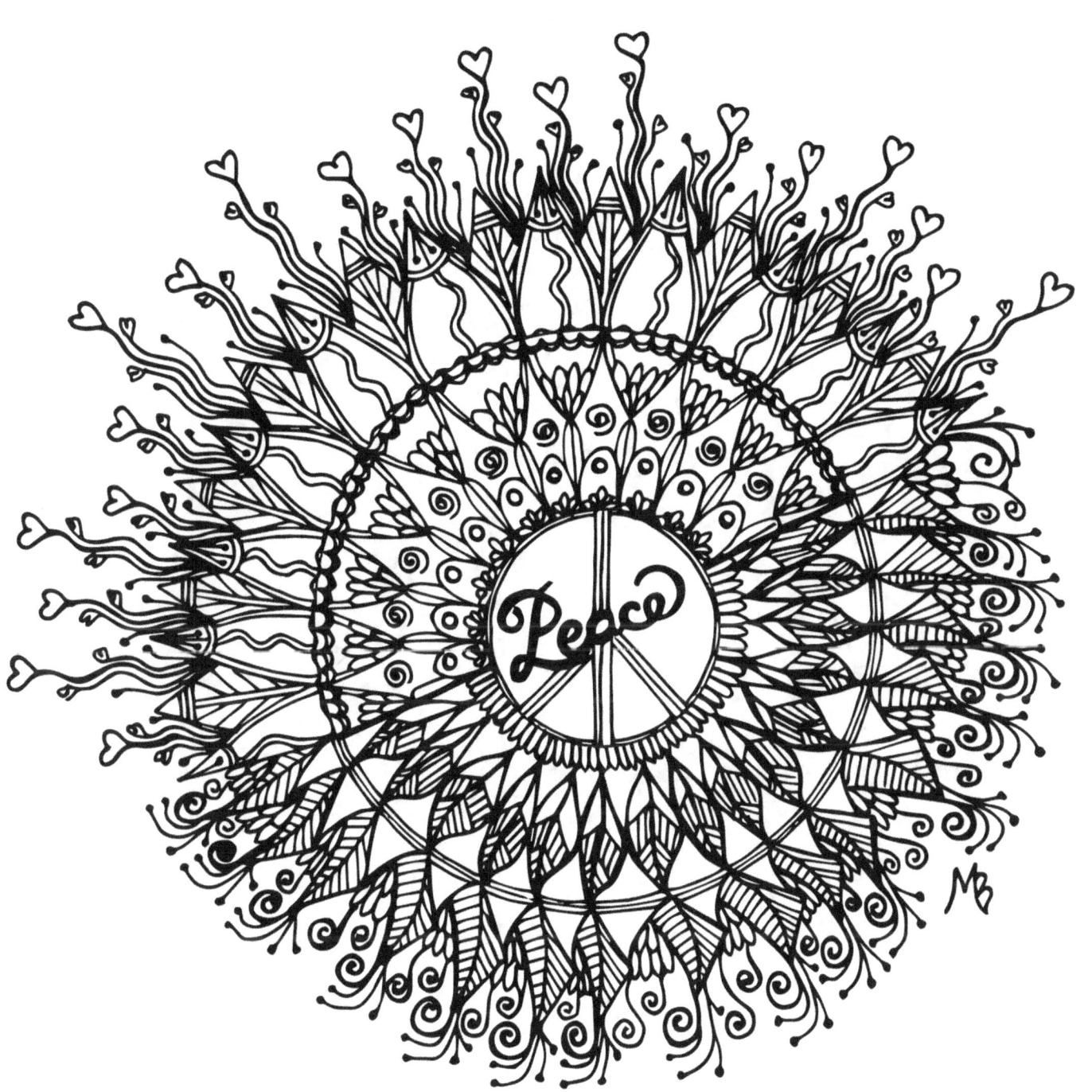

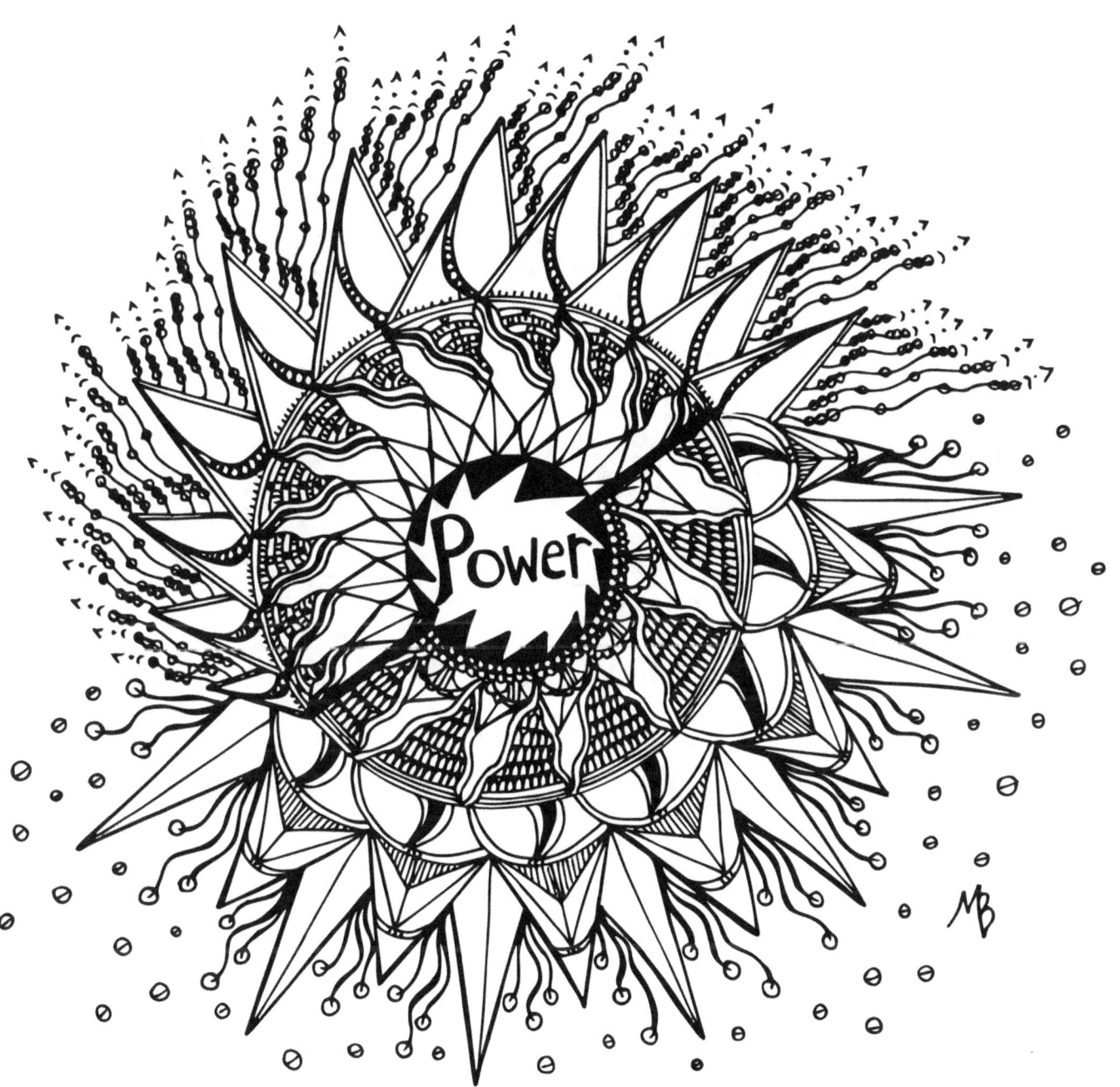

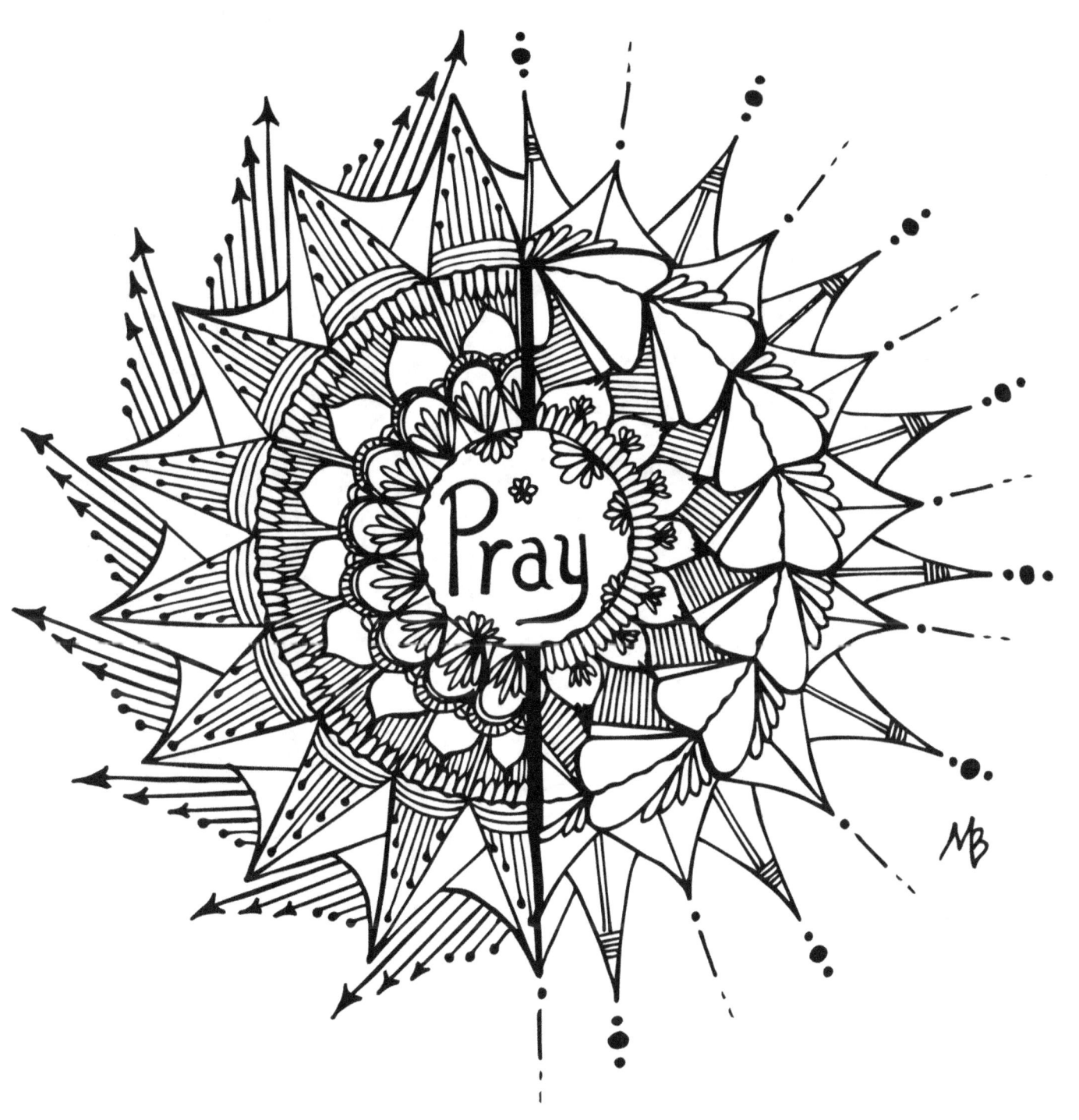

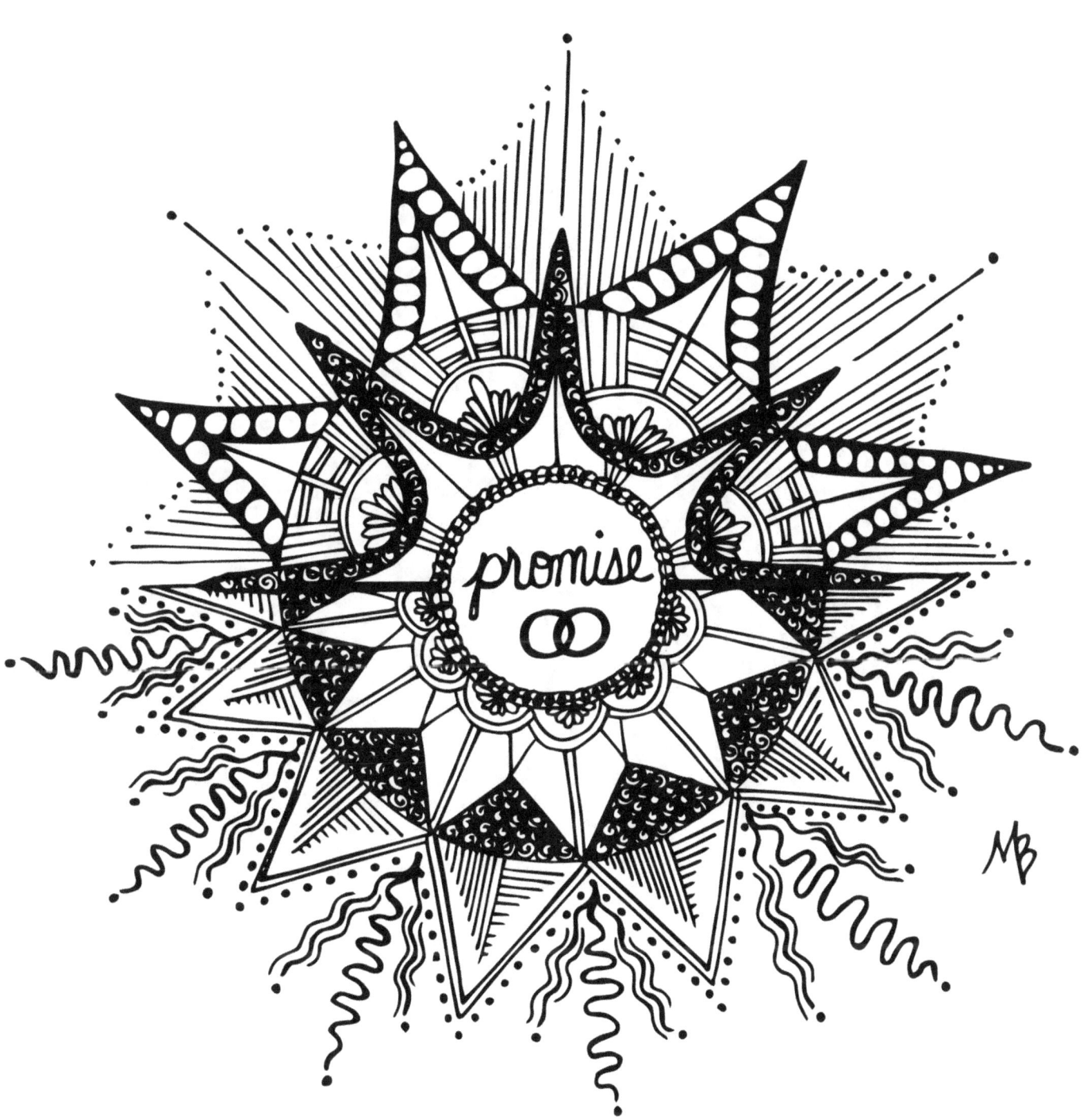

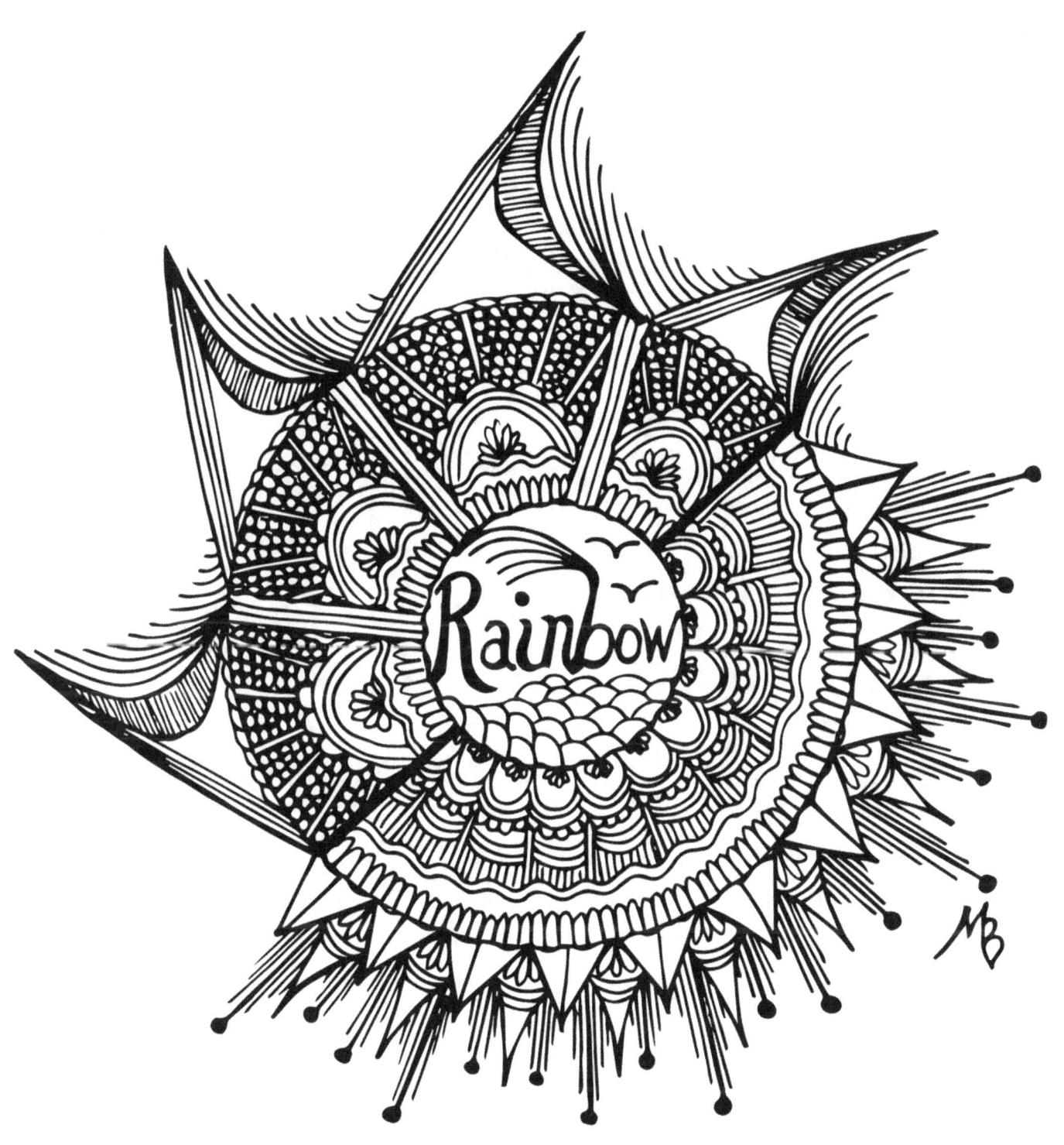

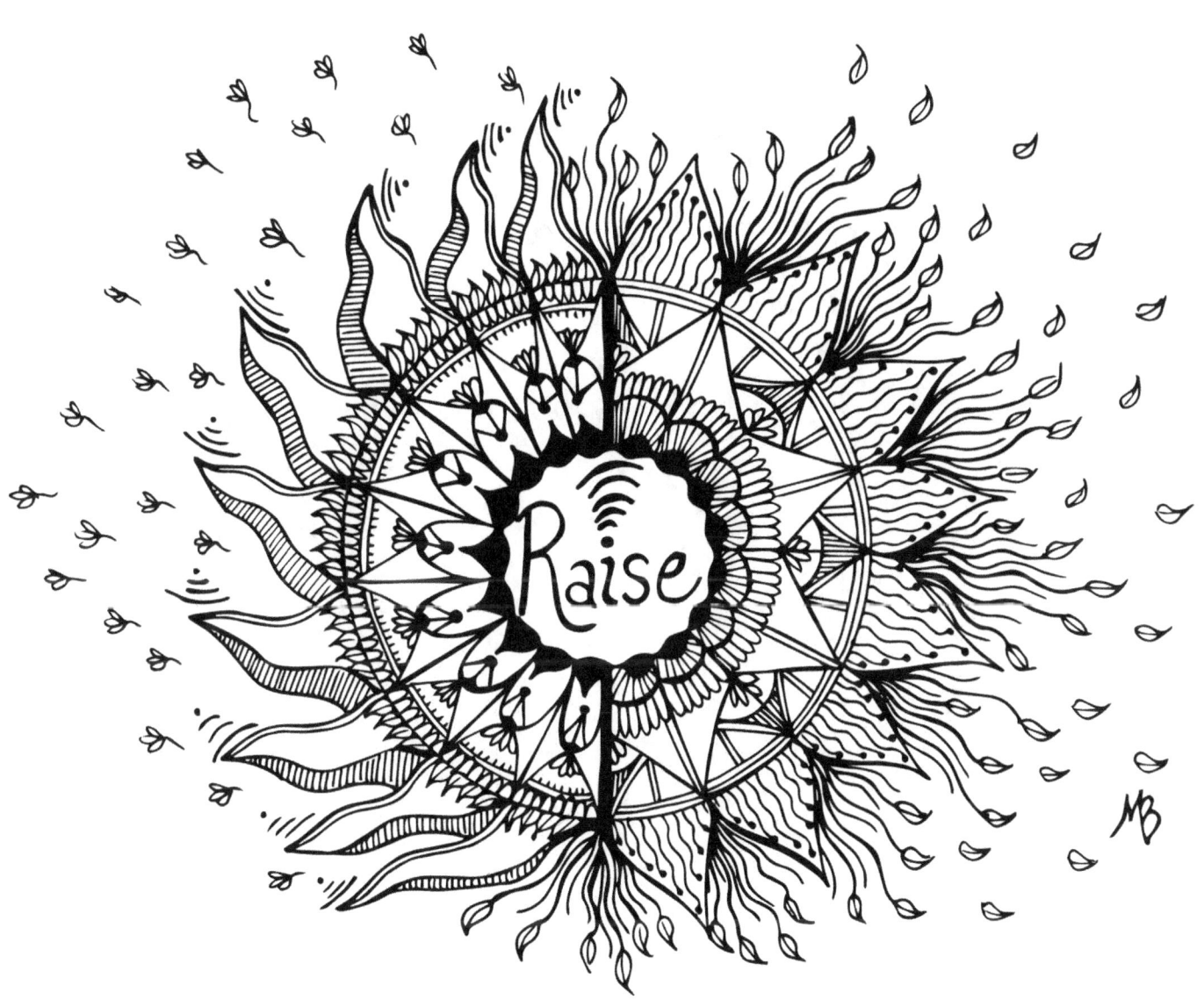

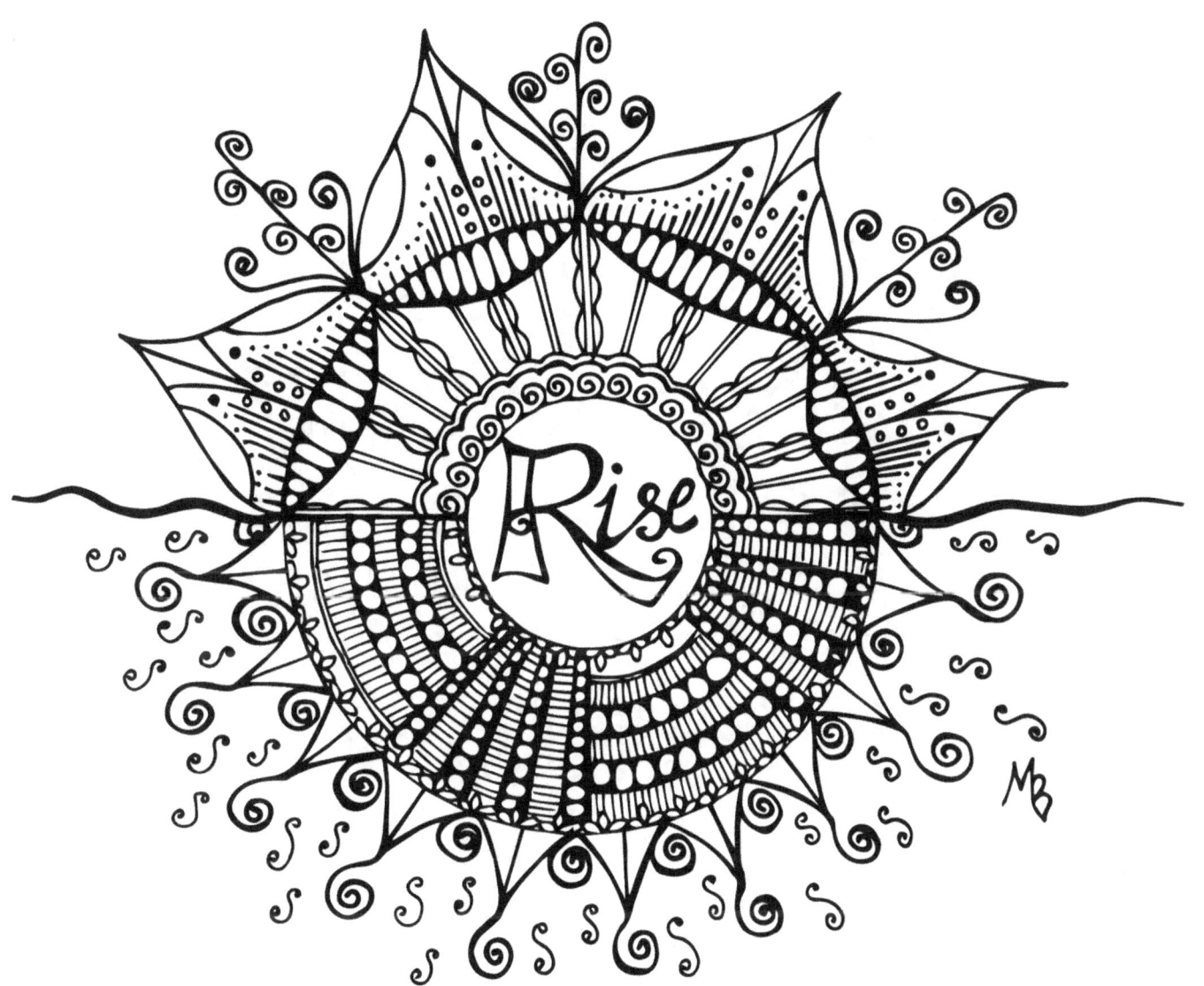

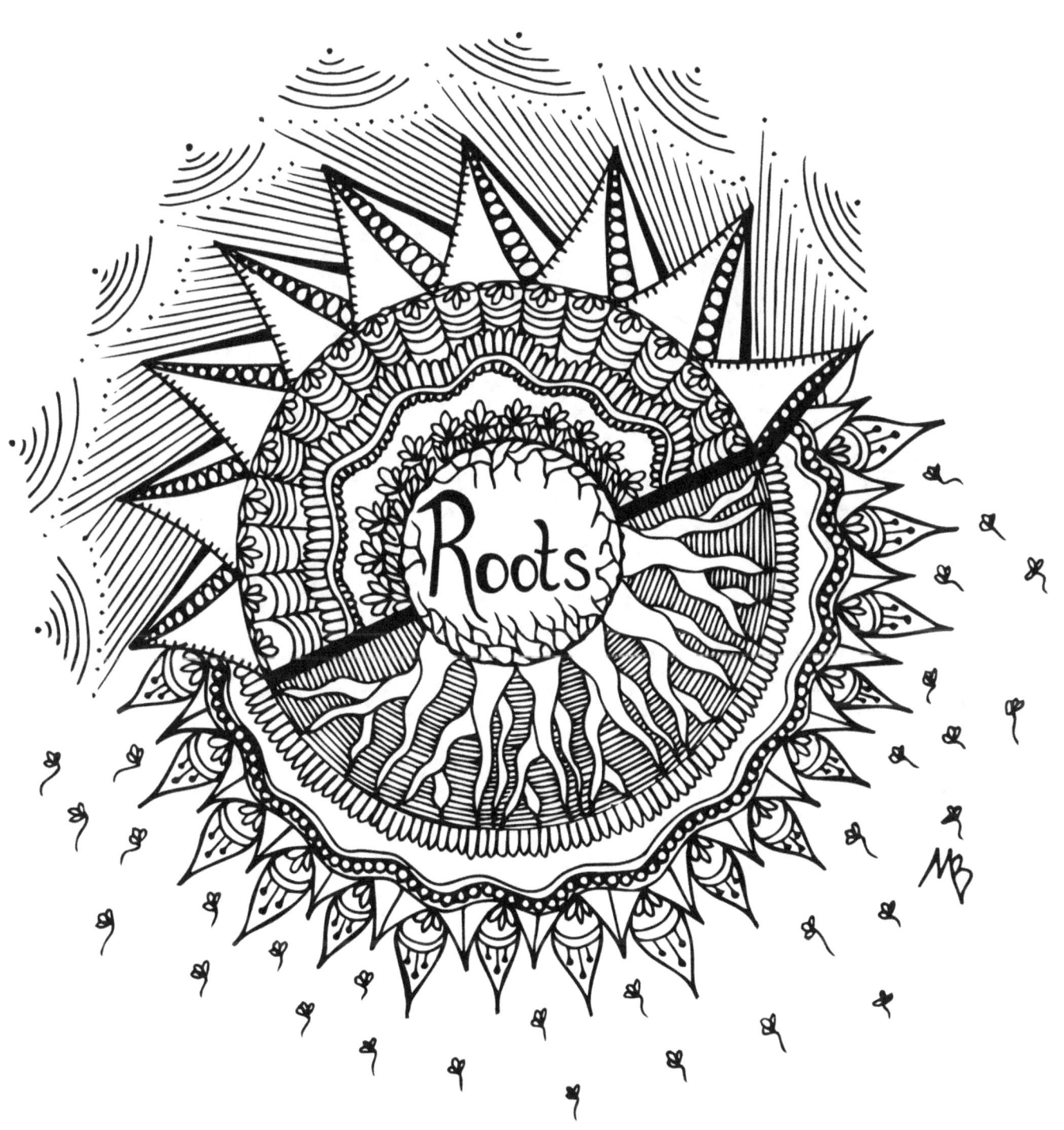

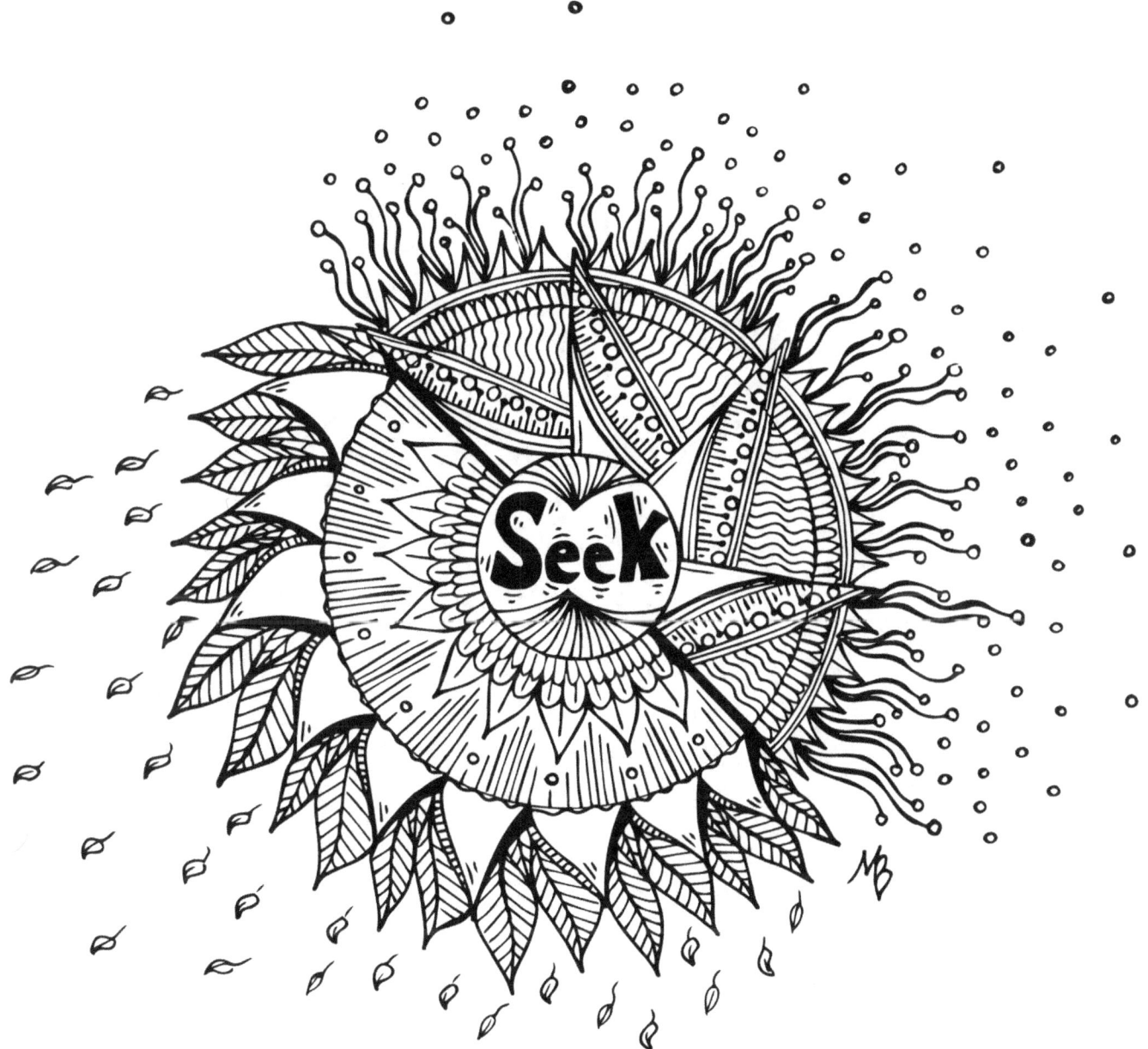

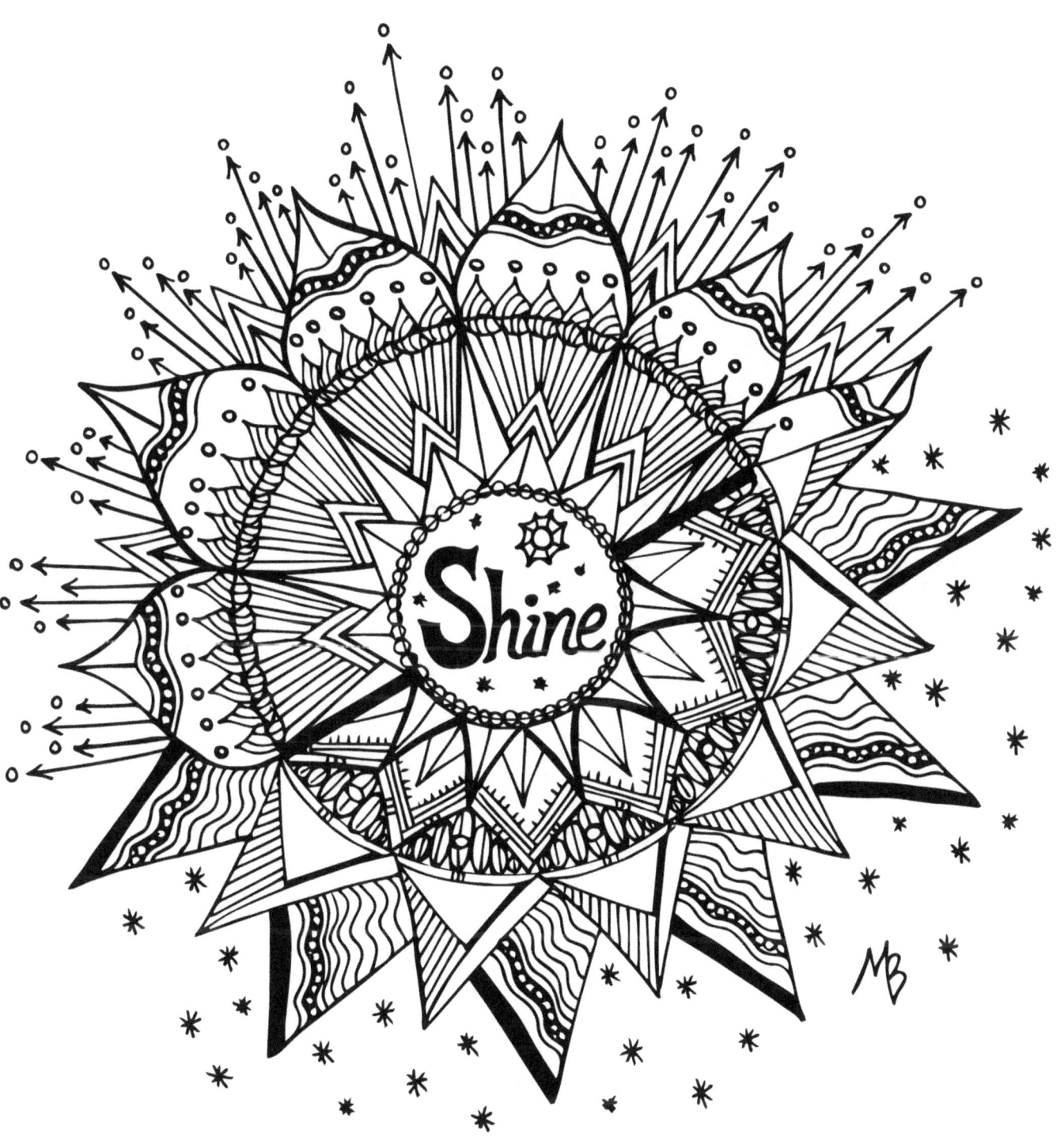

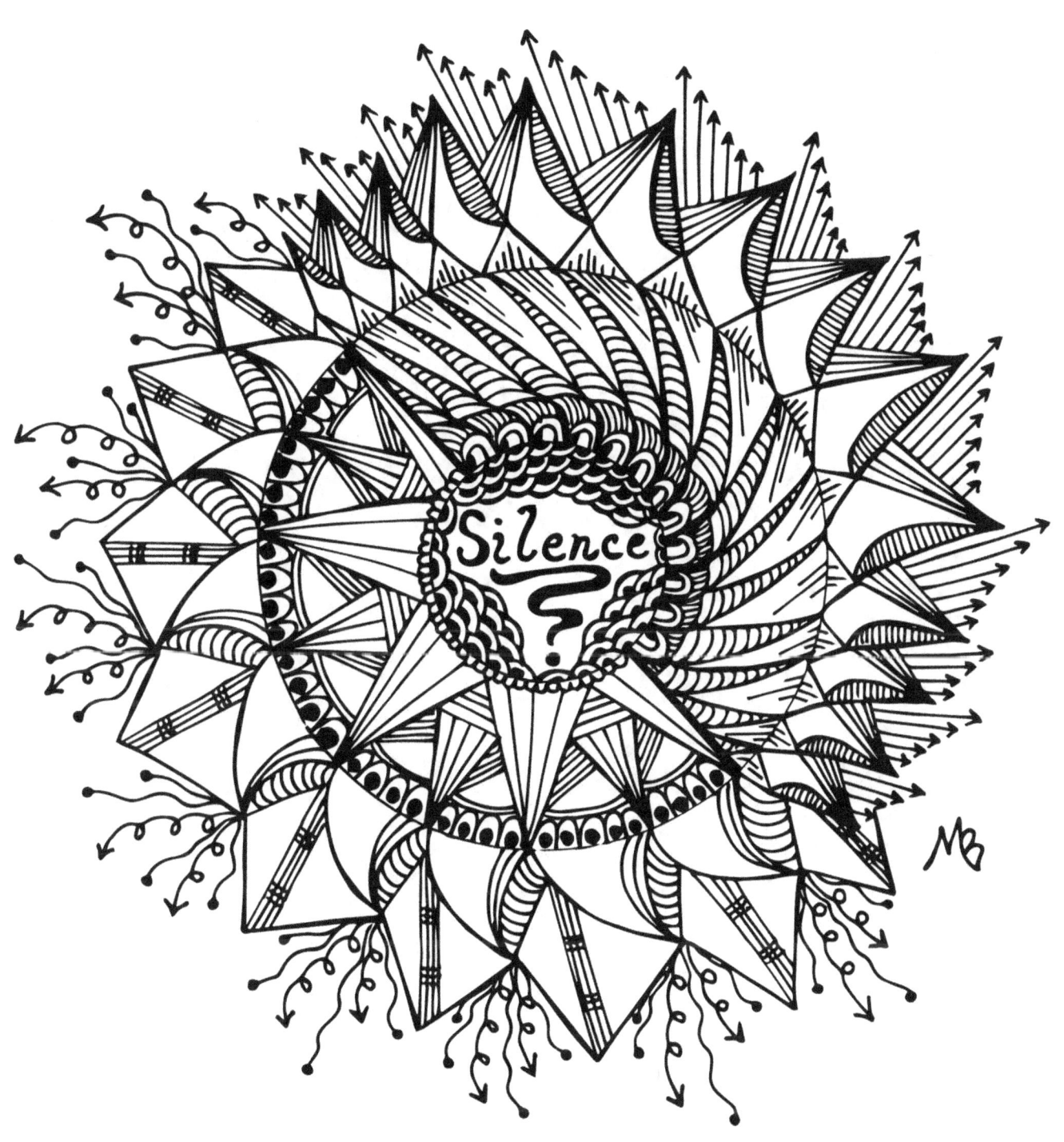

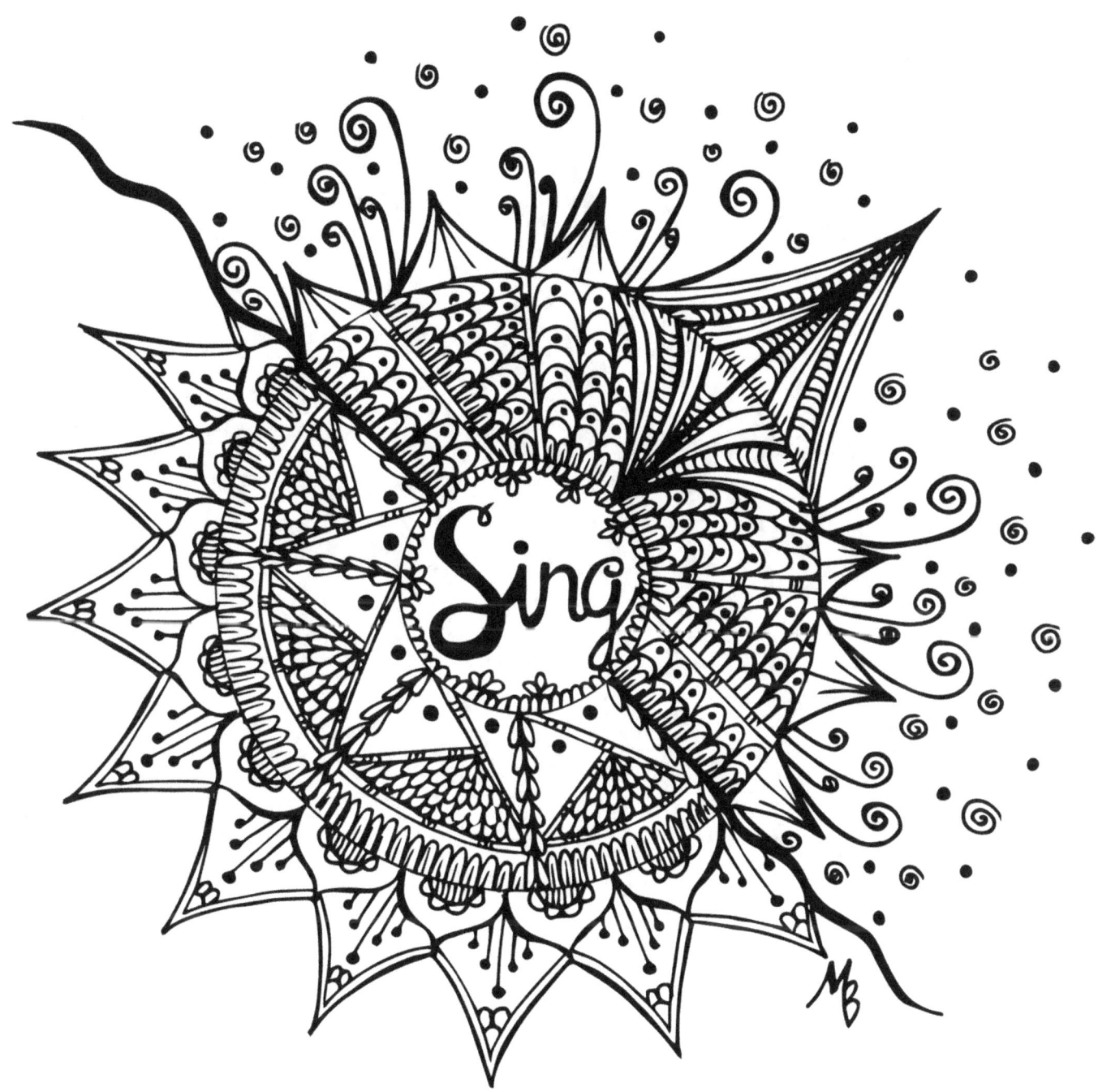

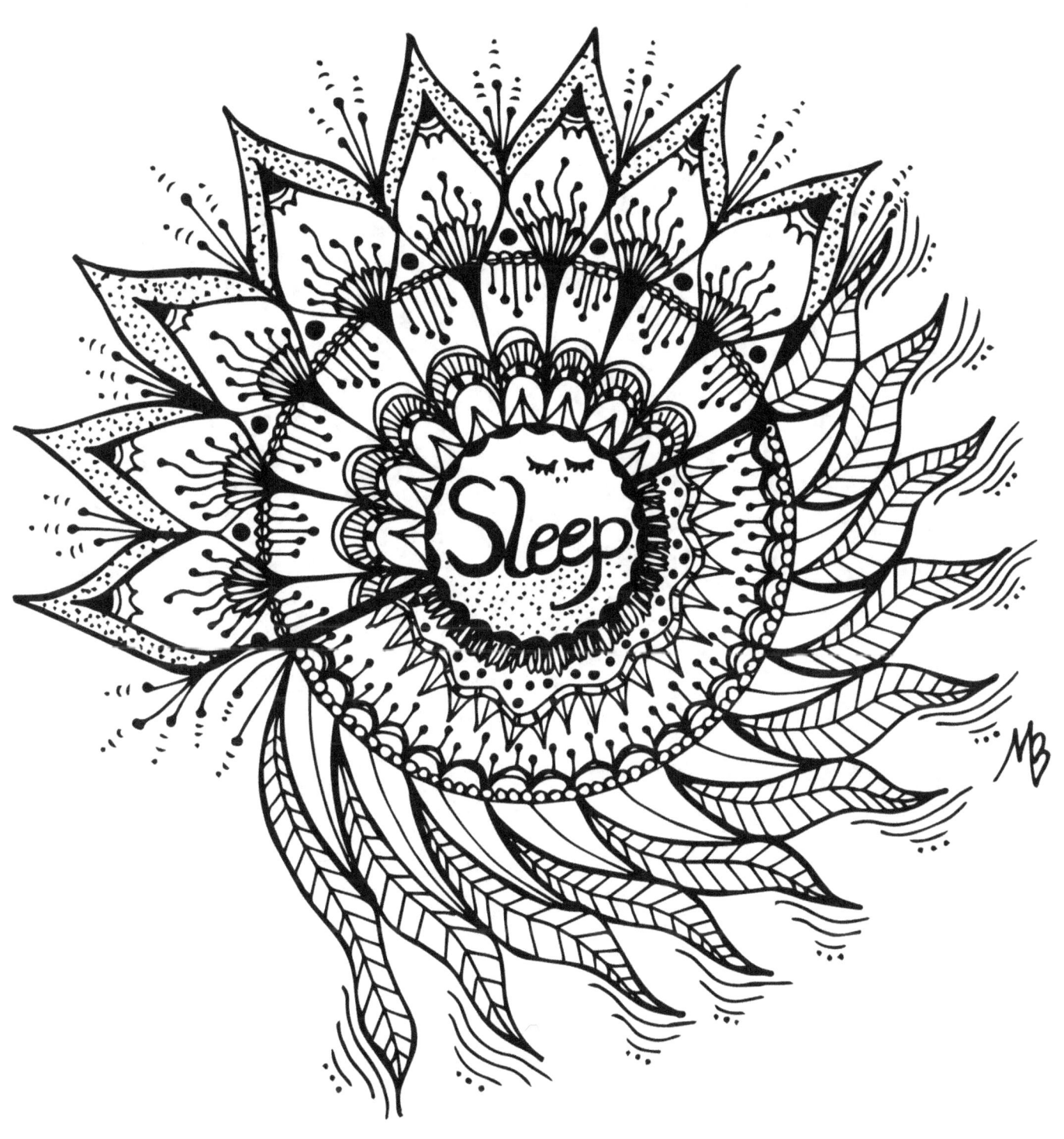

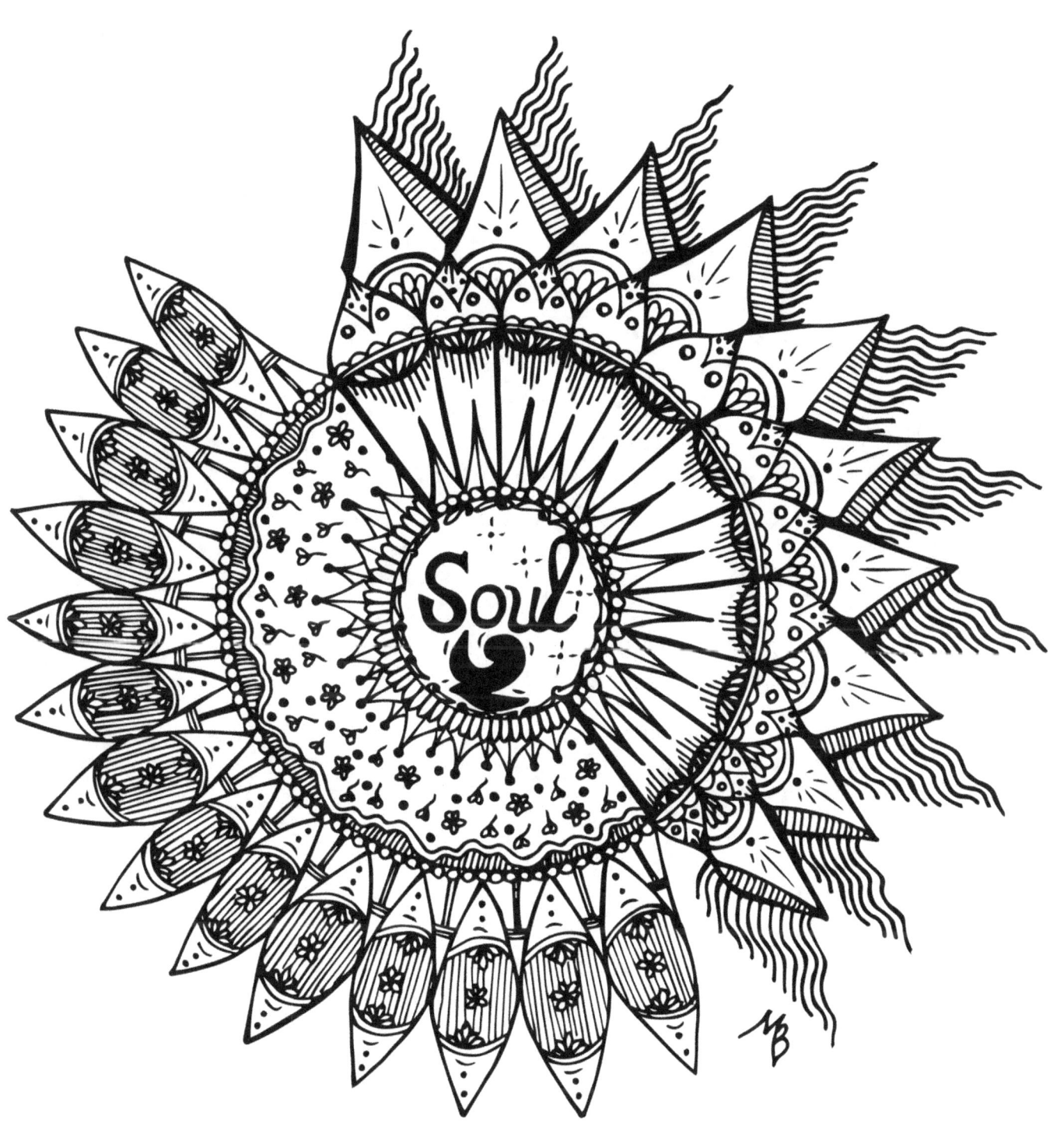

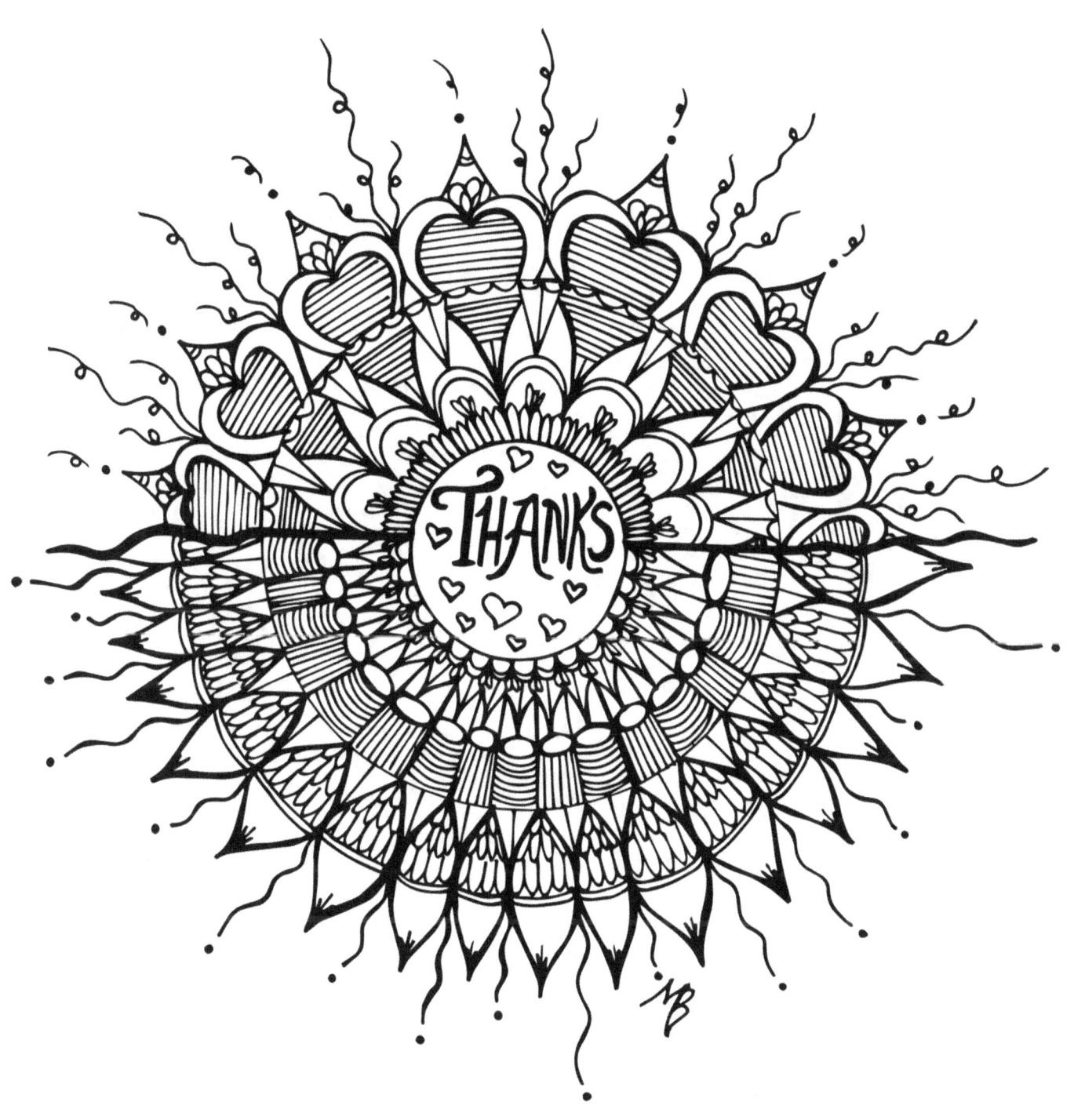

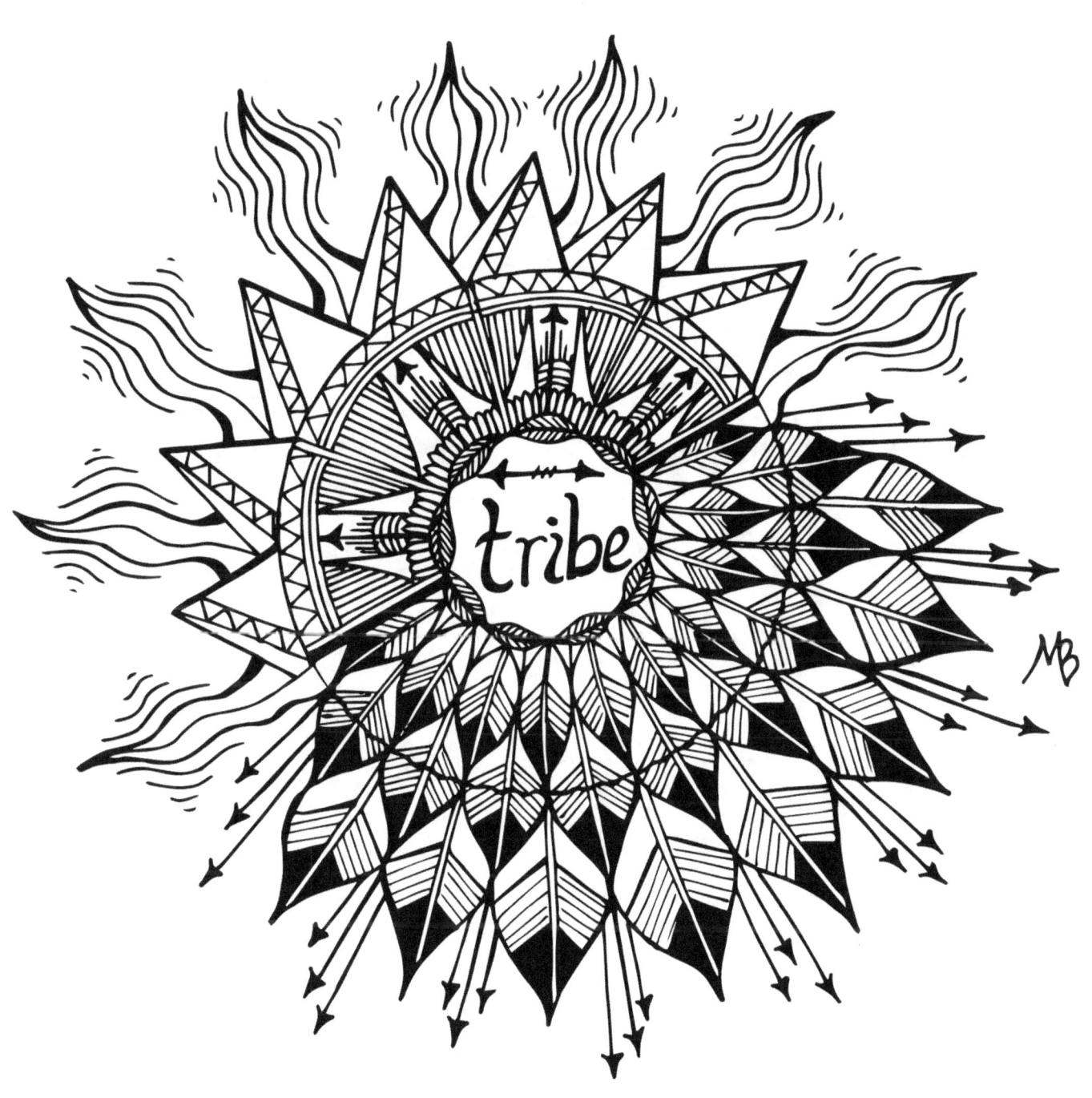

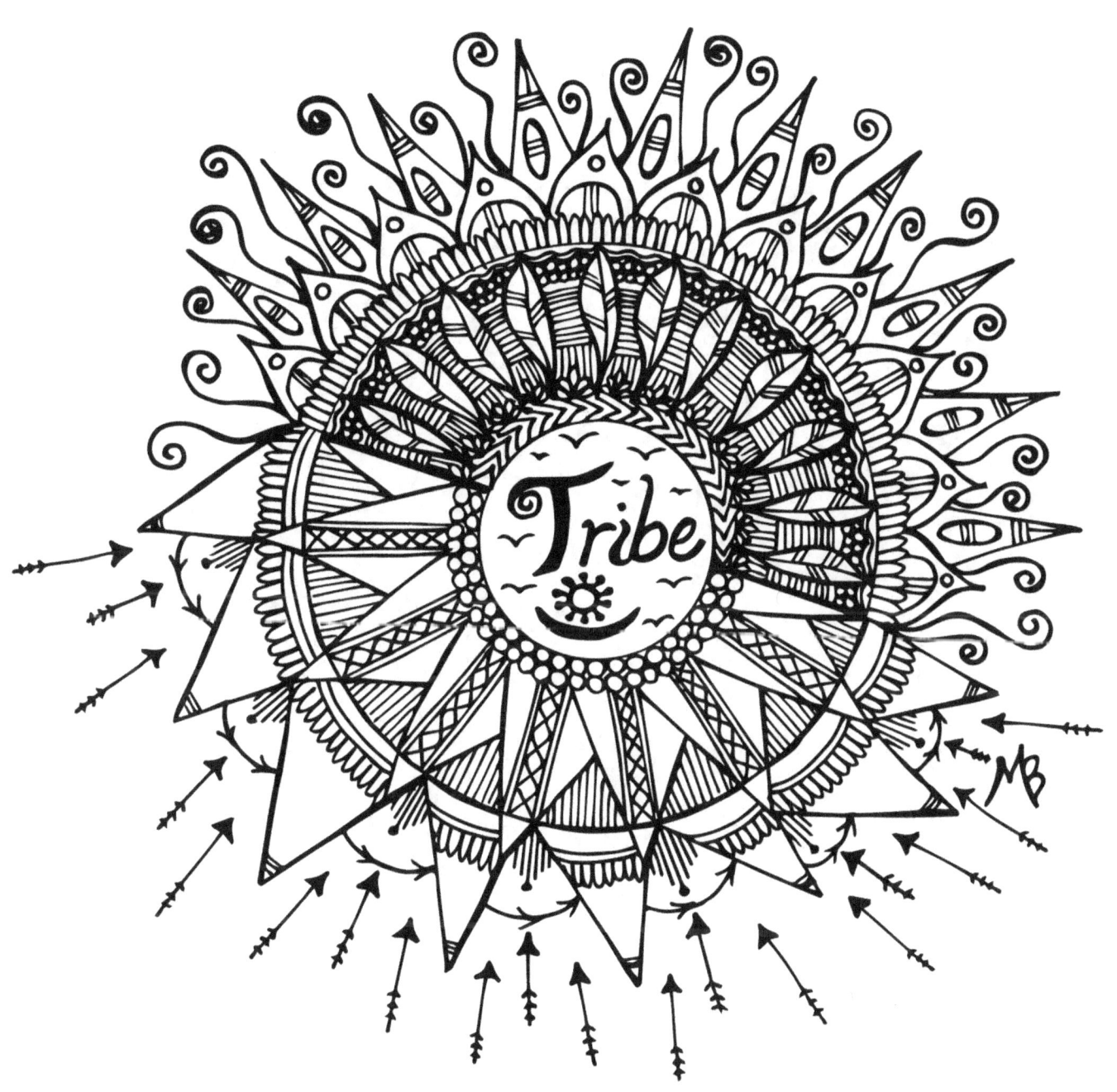

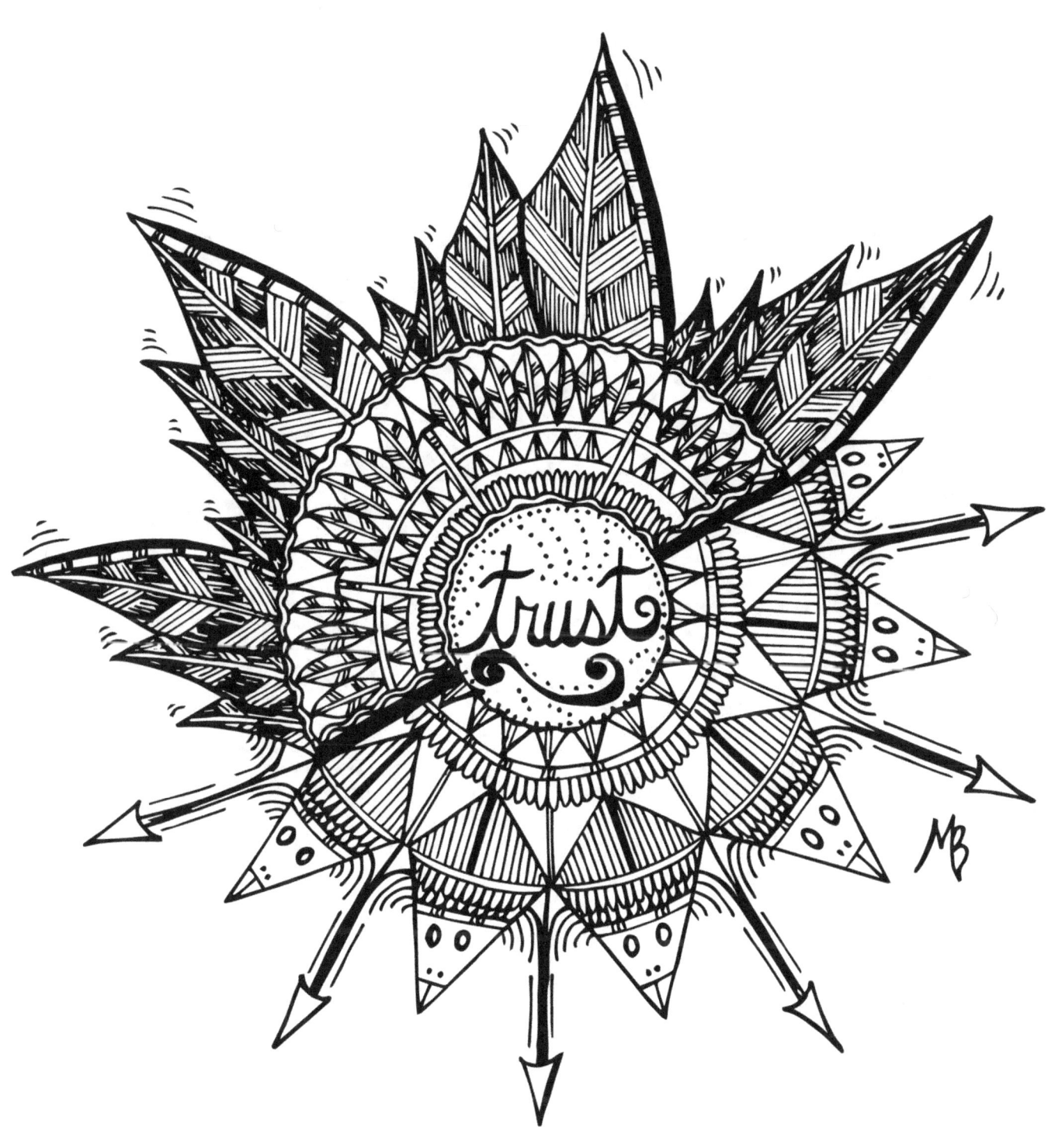

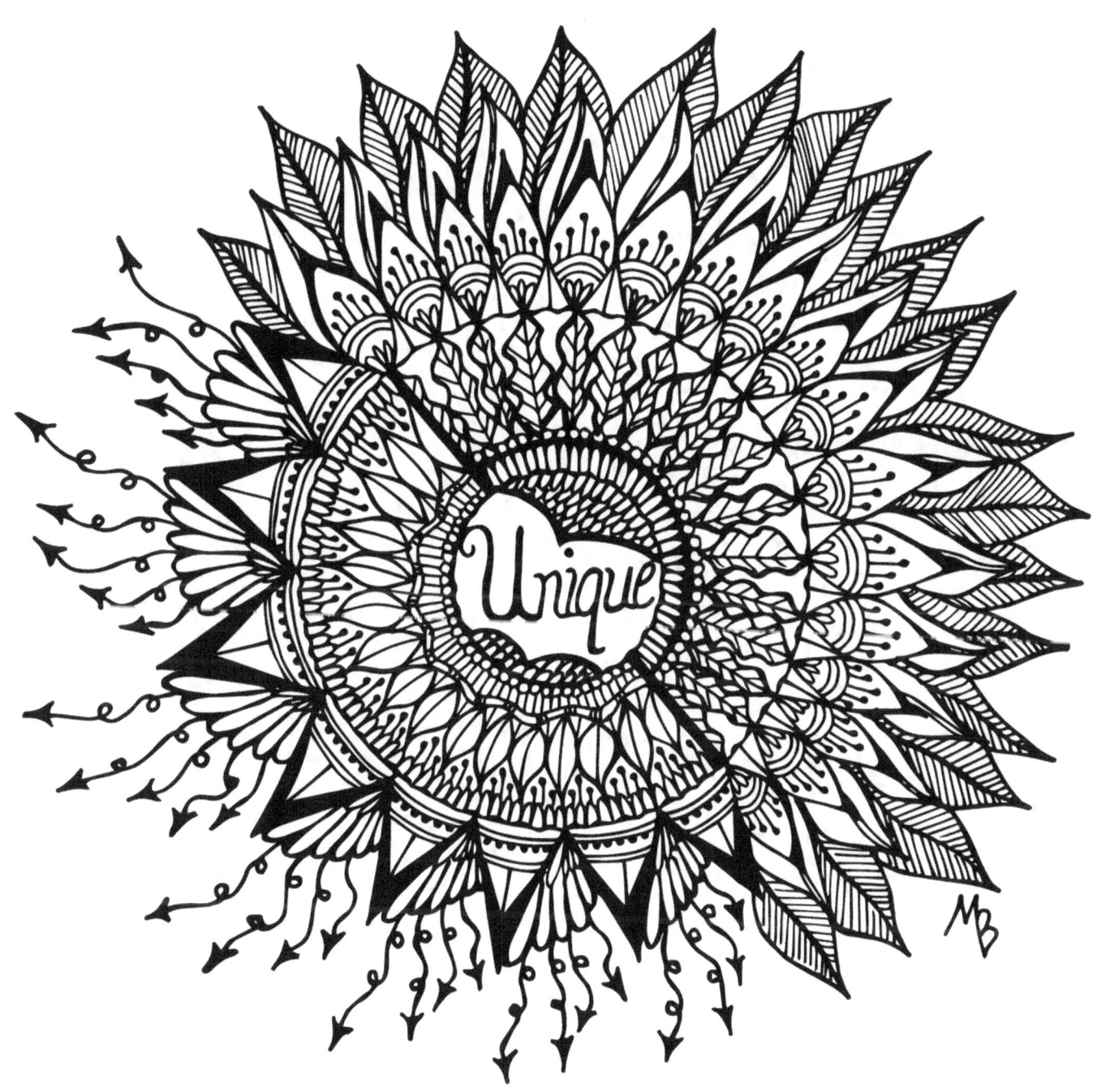

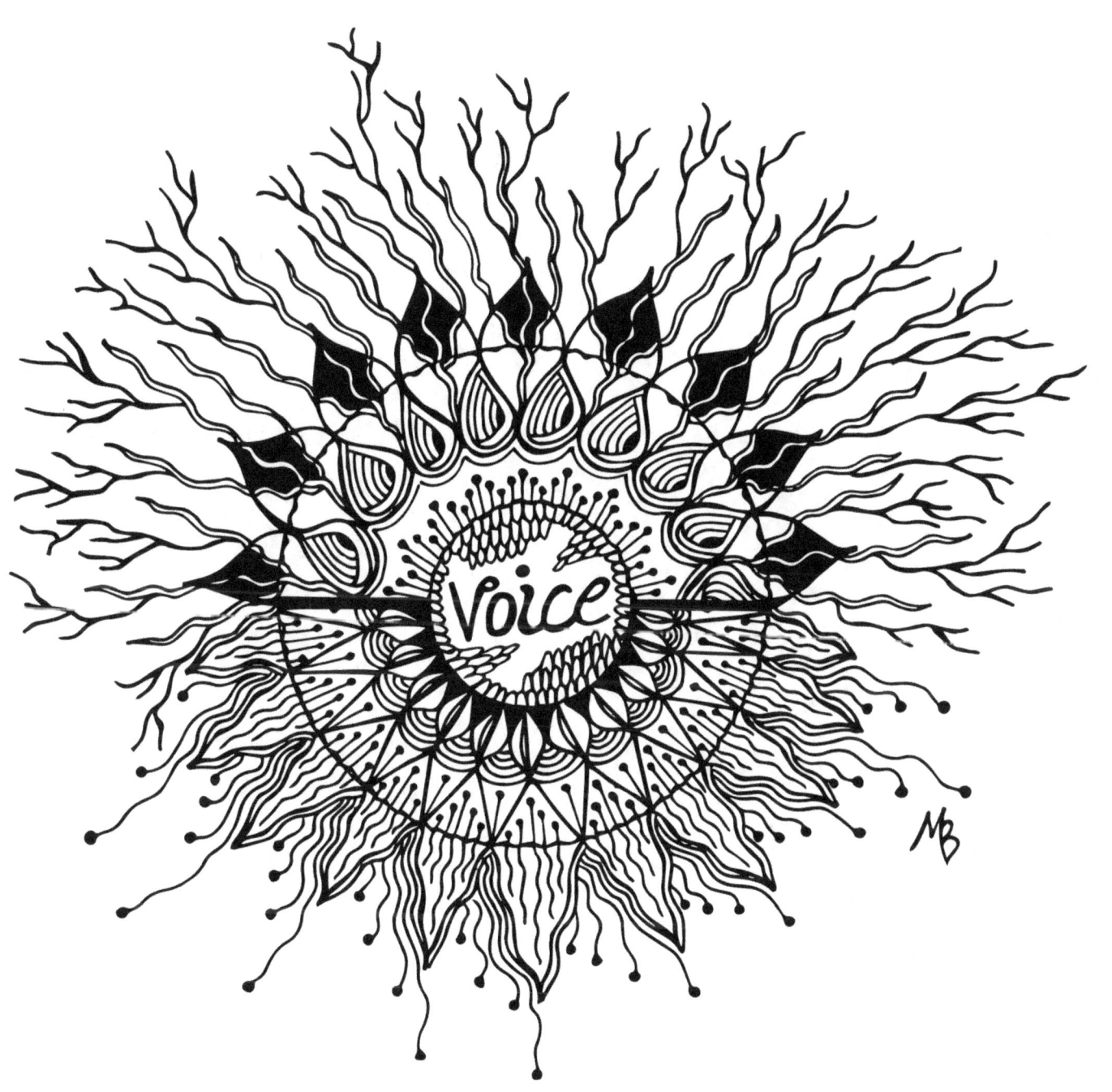

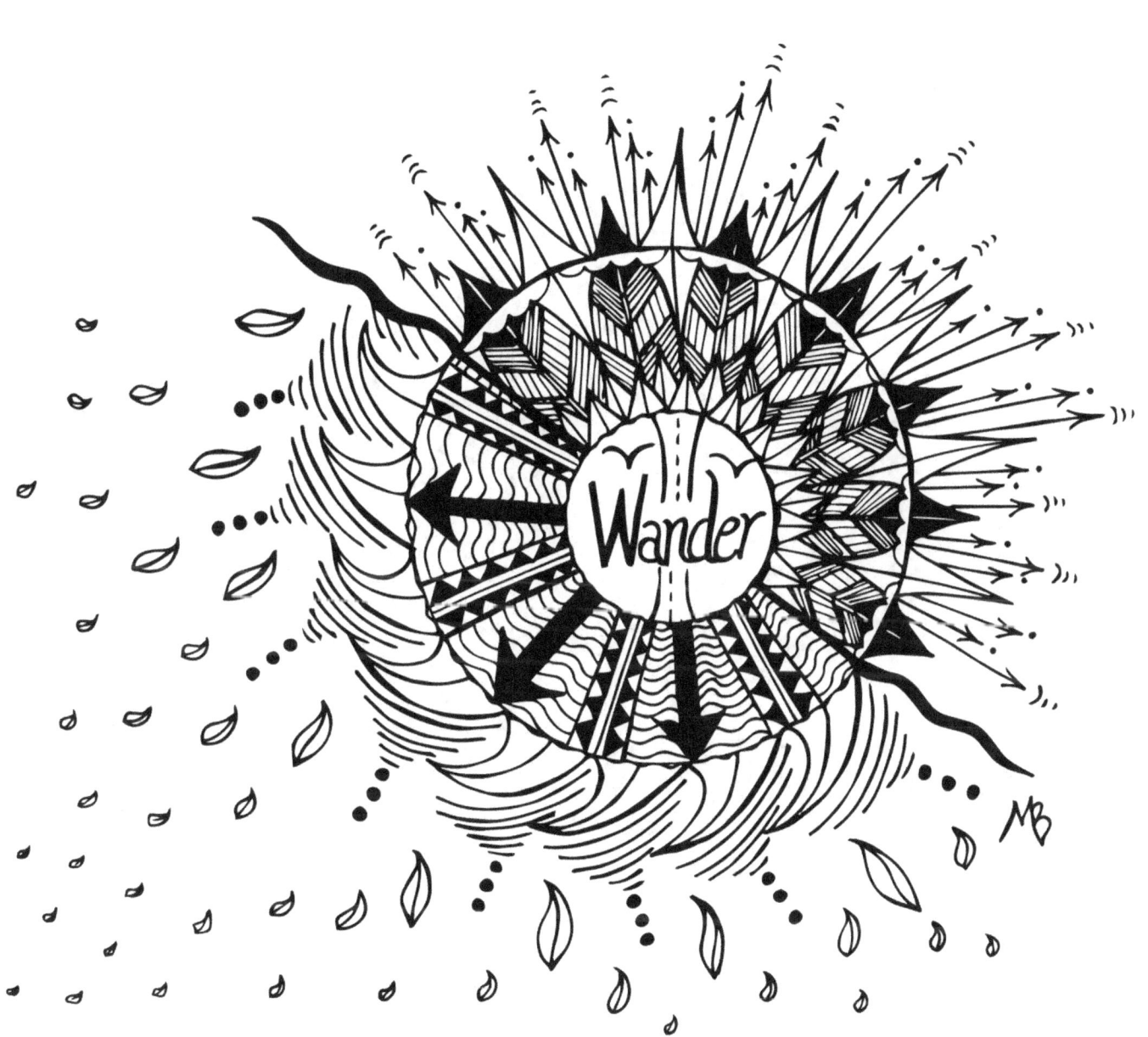

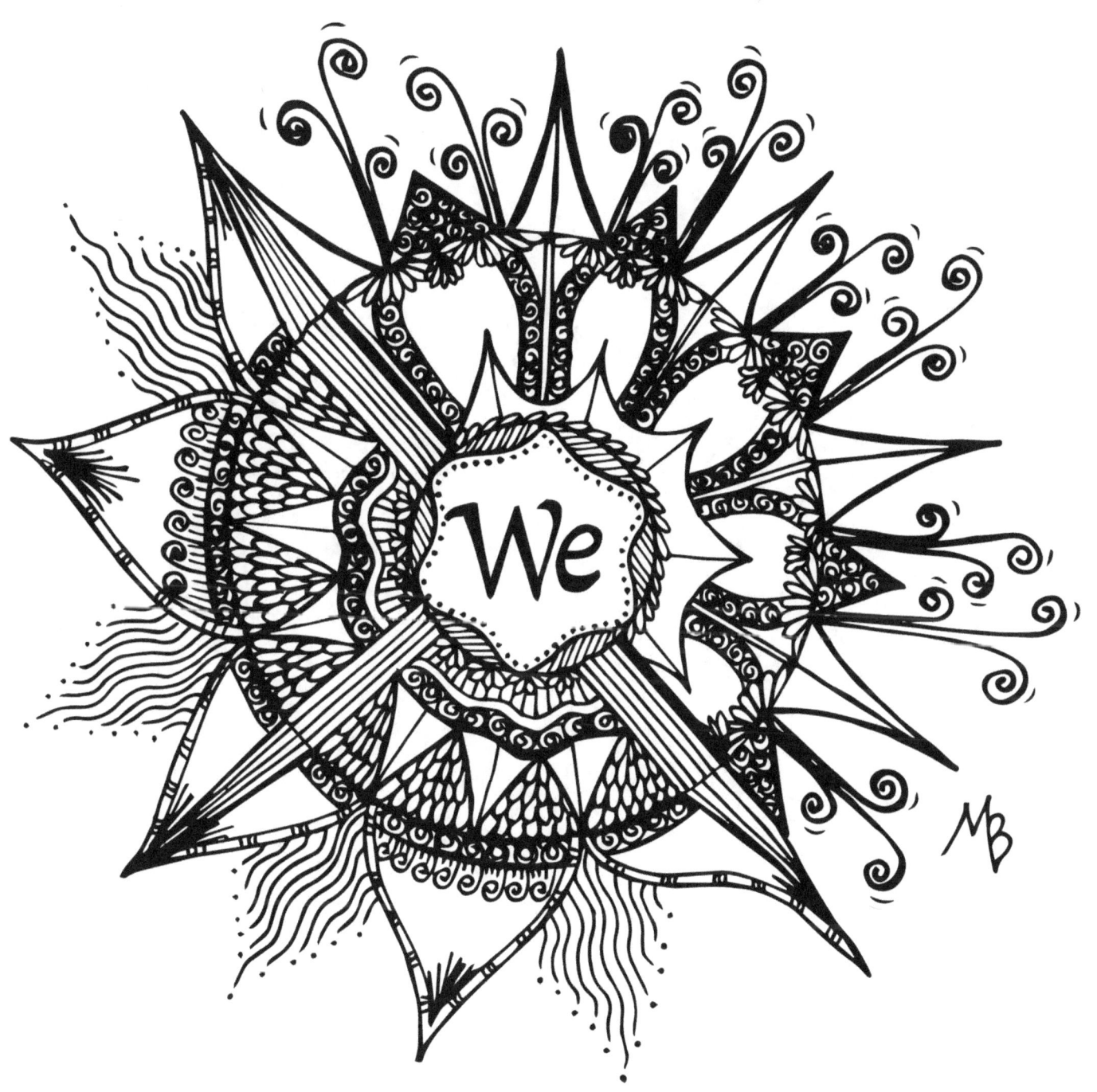

www.ingramcontent.com/pod-product-compliance
Lightning Source LLC
Chambersburg PA
CBHW082212220526
45470CB00010B/3137